C000242315

High Performance Playbook

Win at the Game of Life

DEL DENNEY

Table of Contents

Introduction

On December 25th, 2000 it was a day that changed the rest of my life.

It was Christmas night, and instead of spending time with my family like everyone else in the world, I was at a party in the bad part of my small farm town in Indiana.

Looking back, I had no business being there but that is where my life had led me.

I was in a small apartment of someone that I did not know. I was only 17 years old at the time and as I was in this apartment, with loud music playing, and drugs being freely passed that I noticed everyone in the room.

As I scanned the room, I realized I was the youngest person there. The ages ranged from me being seventeen years old all the way to someone in their 60s. There was a wide spectrum of ages in that room.

And to be very frank, they were all a collection of bad choices. They were all wasting their life away!

That's when I had the biggest moment of clarity in my life.

I had to change what I was doing immediately. I knew that if I kept doing what I was doing, I was going to be just like those people in that room. I knew deep down inside that I wanted more from life than what was in front of me.

At that moment, I stood up and left the party. I never looked back and I knew from that point forward, that I had to make some changes.

Over time, I started reading personal development books. I started changing my habits. I developed a better mindset. I found better friends. I started creating a new life for myself.

I realized that whatever I wanted from life was absolutely possible with the right steps, with the right education, and with the right guidance.

As the Chinese proverb says: "A journey of 1,000 miles begins with a single step" and December 25th, 2000 was my first step towards a better life.

Fast forward to today, and I've lived a life that I am proud of. I can honestly say that if I died today, I have lived a life of purpose. I've been able to travel the world, create precious memories with my family, and have been able to help many people along the way through my coaching programs and seminars.

In fact, by the age of 34 years old, I traveled over a million miles with Delta Airlines from putting on seminars all across the United States and Canada.

What I'm sharing with you in this book isn't anything new. However, it is a curation of actionable items that can help you on your path to being a High Performer. I'm taking 20 years of experience as a practitioner of self-improvement, as a High Performance Coach, and as a motivational speaker, and I'm giving you strategies to improve your life.

I wrote this book for those that want more from life. I wrote this book for those that are looking to break past their limiting beliefs and start reaching their full potential. I wrote this book so you could easily throw it in your backpack, purse, or briefcase and use it whenever you need my help.

I want you to know that these strategies that you find in this book work. You just have to apply it. These strategies are so easy to do, but they are so easy not to do. I've found that successful people have a habit of taking action, and I challenge you to take action on the principles that you are about to learn.

Truly, this is the book that I wish someone handed to me when I started on my path 20 years ago.

Wherever you are on your journey, I'm cheering you on. You may be new to personal development, or you may be a seasoned veteran. Wherever you are, I celebrate you for making a positive step in the right direction. We need more people like you in the world.

This is your time. This is your moment. Are you ready? Of course, you are!

Let's begin.

Section 1:
Gain Clarity in Your Life

Chapter 1: ~~Find~~ Define Your Purpose

"Waste no more time arguing what
a good man should be. Be One."
—**Marcus Aurelius**

Finding our purpose in life is one of the most sought out journeys in human existence. No matter where you live in the world, people are searching for their unique purpose in life. Many have climbed mountains, traveled to far distant parts of the world or have sought out yogis and gurus in their path to enlightenment of purpose.

"What is my purpose in life?" As a life coach, I'm often asked this common question, and I'll share with you what I tell them: **You do not *find* your purpose, you *define* your purpose.**

You, my friend, get to dictate what your purpose is in life. You get to proactively define how you will show up in the world and how you'll give back.

Steve Jobs said it best: *"Your time is limited, so don't waste it living someone else's life. Don't be trapped by dogma—which is living with the results of other people's thinking. Don't let the noise of others' opinions drown out your own inner voice. And most important, have the courage to follow your heart and intuition."*

To add to that thought, I would also like to warn about dogma. Just because your parents had a particular profession doesn't mean you have to follow that profession. Just because you were raised a certain way doesn't mean you have to raise your children a certain way. Just because you were raised with one particular theological ideology doesn't mean you have to continue down that path.

You, my friend, get to define yourself.

==

The Philosophy of Ikigai

In our path of defining our purpose, we are going to use a Japanese philosophy called Ikigai.

Ikigai (pronounced Ick-ee-guy) is the Japanese secret to a long, happy and fulfilling life.

Ikigai is best understood in the context of East Asian culture, relating to the concepts of mindfulness or introspection, these being critical practices in life to reaching your full potential.

The philosophy of Ikigai may be considered as *working in a state of flow in line with your life purpose.*

This philosophy of life comes from the Okinawa Islands where the people there appear to live a longer life than most people in the world, with an average lifespan of 84 years old and some people there even reaching 120+ years of age! One of the cornerstones of the Okinawans' lifestyle is that they have defined their purpose in life through the philosophy of Ikigai.

Studies have shown Japanese longevity to be closely related to their diet and health practices, but new studies on Japanese philosophy have shown life fulfillment through Ikigai as a key component to their longevity.

Your understanding of your life's purpose and acting upon it can contribute to your longevity.

However, Ikigai can be found in every place on Earth. You don't need to live in Okinawa, Japan to define your purpose in life.

Everyone's purpose is unique—it's based on your defined values, your personal history, your beliefs and your personality.

Defining your own Ikigai is said to bring fulfillment, happiness and may even make you live longer.

So, how do you define your purpose in life using this Japanese philosophy?

You can define your Ikigai by following these simple steps and answering these four fundamental questions:

- What do you love?
- What are you good at?
- What can you get paid for?
- What does the world need?

What do you love?

When defining your purpose, consider what you loved doing or dreamed of doing when you were a child? Or what activities do you now do in your spare time that make you happy?

To be happy and successful, we must do what we love. We have to find something which makes us lose the sense of time, which most excites us and which helps us be "in the flow" state.

If you are searching for a job, make sure that the next job you get is something you would love doing every day.

If you already have a job at which you are not happy, or you hate to go to it every day, then start looking for another job. Life is short. Don't stick with a job that makes you unhappy.

If you have a business, you must be able to control the flow of activities in such a way that you will enjoy running your business every day.

Do what you love. That's the first key component in defining your purpose.

What are you good at?

To answer the second question, "What are you good at?", try to be as objective as possible.

You probably think you have a clear idea regarding the things you are good at, and to some extent you're probably right.

But I would also challenge you to ask other people's opinions about your skills and talents.

They may provide you with valuable and honest feedback. Ask your friends, your colleagues and your employer for their opinions. Give them permission to be fully honest with you, and don't react emotionally to what they say. Use this as data and not as a personal judgment.

Think about some activities at which you outperformed others in the past, those which came naturally to you, the things you were praised for, admired or even envied.

If you're lucky, you may discover that it's already exactly what you're doing in your current vocation.

If you're not lucky in that regard, it may mean you are working in the wrong field, in which case it is advisable to make a plan to switch careers, either by jumping to another job or by starting to work in your free time in the field in which you are the most skilled. Maybe you should even start a business.

There may be many things you are good at, but when it comes to your profession, you have to choose the one you also love to do, what the world needs, and the one for which you can get paid.

That's key in defining your Ikigai.

What can you get paid for?

Today, you can create income from almost anything if you have the right tools and strategies.

A list of the best-paid jobs in the world may be easy to find on the internet; however, if you're just chasing money, happiness will probably not follow.

According to Japanese philosophy, you cannot have Ikigai if your finances are in jeopardy. Find a job that you love which you are good at and that keeps your finances where they need to be according to the lifestyle that you desire.

What does the world need?

Last, but not least, the question for defining your Ikigai or your life's purpose is "What does the world need?"

Your purpose is not only about focusing inward but also outward.

While focusing on your passion, money and profession, also focus on the people you serve. If we add value to other people and contribute to improving the world, chances are we'll be taken care of, too.

Defining your purpose is not complete without this outward dimension. Our happiness is interrelated with the value we add to others.

As famous actor Will Smith said: "The only sustainable mission throughout your existence is to improve lives."

We all have to analyze the needs of the people around us and respond to them, improving our communities, and ultimately, the world.

You cannot have Ikigai without feeling how important your work is for this world and those around you.

So let's recap these four questions to define your life's purpose:

- What do you love?
- What are you good at?
- What can you get paid for?
- What does the world need?

Now let's break this down a little bit further and see how these questions are interrelated.

Here's an interesting fact—according to Japanese philosophy, the intersection of what you are good at and what you can be paid for is your *profession*.

The intersection of what the world needs and what you love is your *mission*.

The intersection of what you love and what you are good at is your *passion*.

And the intersection of what the world needs and what you can be paid for is your *vocation*.

Finally, Ikigai, your *purpose in life*, will be given by the intersection of your *profession*, your *mission*, your *passion* and your *vocation*.

Ikigai (Your Purpose) is when all four areas overlap.

Passion and *Mission* are not enough to help you have a fulfilling life. You also need to have a career or vocation *and* get a paycheck.

Likewise, happiness is much more than simply having a career and a paycheck.

For achieving *purpose* in life, we need all four areas met. We need to work on something which we love, are good at, pays well, and is something the world needs.

In essence, that is how we define our life's *purpose*.

Use this framework to define your own individual life's *purpose*.

Take Action:

- **Set time aside this week to define your purpose using the framework of Ikigai.**
- **Ask yourself: "What do you love? What are you good at? What can you get paid for? What does the world need?"**

Chapter 2: How to Create Harmony in Your Life

"How long are you going to wait before
you demand the best for yourself?"
—Epictetus

With so many demands today, it can be challenging to live a happy and balanced life. Some people are succeeding at work, but they sacrifice their relationships at home. Some people have incredible relationships at home, but they have anxiety because they haven't focused enough on their finances. Some people are succeeding financially, but they're overweight because they haven't focused on their health.

True *High Performers* are people who consistently sustain success at a high level without sacrificing the important moments in life.

Here's the thing—I want you to succeed in all areas of your life. I want you to have a happy marriage. I want you to succeed at work. I want you to have fun. I want you to become the best version of yourself.

And one way to help you on your path to a happy and fulfilled life is to consistently monitor where you stand in key categories in your life that I like to call *Areas of Focus*.

AREAS OF FOCUS

There is a quote from T.S. Monson that says, "When performance is measured, performance improves. When performance is measured and reported back, the rate of performance *accelerates*." My goal is to help accelerate your growth and happiness, and we'll do that by measuring these areas:

- Health
- Romance
- Relationships
- Mission
- Finances
- Recreation
- Spiritual
- Personal Growth

Health

I believe that health is wealth. We can have all the money in the world, but if we are lying sick in bed all the time, then what is the point of being wealthy? When our health is optimized, it allows us to live a more vibrant life.

How is your health? Do you have the physical and mental stamina needed every day to overcome life's challenges? Are you taking time for yourself to recharge your batteries? Are you receiving the proper nutrition? Are you getting the rest your body needs?

On a scale of 1 to 10, rank yourself on how well you're doing in the category of *Health*.

Romance

We all have a desire to love and to be loved, and when we find that special person in our life, it makes us feel as if we are walking on a cloud. It's important to have someone in our life worth fighting for. It's important to have a physical connection. We must often communicate these three words: "I love you."

So how are you doing with your love life? Do you have a deep connection with your significant other? Do you trust your significant other? Are you attentive to your partner's needs physically and emotionally?

On a scale of 1 to 10, rank yourself on how well you're doing in that category of *Romance*.

Relationships

We crave human connection. As humans, it's ingrained in us to be a part of a tribe. A thousand years ago, being connected to a tribe was a part of our survival. It was in the tribe where we had safety. We had safety from the animals that might attack us and safety from the other tribes, as well. If we were vanquished from the tribe, it meant fending for ourselves and a death sentence. We needed to be connected to our tribe.

Today, we may not have tribes, but we have people in our lives who we value and with whom want to stay connected. These may include close friends, family and coworkers.

How is your social circle doing these days? Do you have real and authentic relationships? Do you give more than you receive? Are you a good friend? Are you visiting regularly with family members?

On a scale of 1 to 10, rank yourself on how well you're doing in the category of *Relationships*.

Mission

When we define our purpose and we are living each day intentionally, we can find real fulfillment in our work. When we are giving back to the world, that's when we feel joy. When we are in alignment with our Ikigai, that's when we are in alignment with our mission.

Have you defined your purpose? Are you living in congruence with your mission? Are you giving back to the world? Are you doing your best work?

On a scale of 1 to 10, rank yourself with how well you're doing in the category of *Mission*.

Finances

In my personal opinion, I don't believe our formal education gives us a proper financial education. That's why we see so many people living paycheck to paycheck, and many people are unhappy with their jobs.

When we start understanding the rules of money and become better stewards of our money, we will start to breathe a little easier. Knowing the difference between an asset and liability should be taught in our schools, but for the most part it is not.

We have to get a handle on our finances. As Benjamin Franklin once said, "Beware of expenses. A small leak will sink a great ship."

How are you doing financially? Are you saving your money? Are you investing your money? Do you have enough money for your needs? Do you have a healthy bank account?

On a scale of 1 to 10, rank yourself with how well you're doing in the category of *Finances*.

Recreation

We aren't put on this earth just to work and then die. We are meant to have fun and live a life of vibrancy. My mother always told me, "I work to live. I don't live to work." Too many people are all work and no play. We need to take the time to play!

Think about if you were exercising hard and going to the gym every day without any breaks. What would eventually happen? You would probably hurt a muscle or tweak your back. Just like our bodies, our minds need a break, too.

I find that when I take a break from the grind and go do something fun, I come back with more creativity and a better attitude.

How about you? Are you taking time for yourself to have fun? Do you have any hobbies outside of work? Are you giving yourself time for the things you love?

On a scale of 1 to 10, rank yourself with how well you're doing in the category of *Recreation*.

Spiritual

I don't care if you are Christian, Buddhist, Muslim or believe in a God or not...What I care about is that you are in alignment with your own spiritual beliefs. If we profess to believe in one thing but our actions demonstrate another, that can lead to much mental and spiritual anguish.

Are you living in accordance with your spiritual beliefs? Do your actions demonstrate your beliefs? Do you have peace of mind?

On a scale of 1 to 10, rank yourself on how well you're doing in the category of *Spiritual*.

Personal Growth

Here's a fact that you may not know about me: I did not graduate from college. I don't have one college credit to my name. Although I don't have a formal education, I'm very well educated.

Whenever I want to become better at any part of my life, I read a book, take a course, or seek out a coach or mentor. This has helped me grow into the person I am today.

I used to think that because I didn't have a college degree to my name that it was a bad thing, but what I now realize is that wasn't true at all. Every day, I strive to be better than I was yesterday. Every day, I take the time to focus on my personal growth.

But here's where a lot of people go wrong. Many people graduate from college and stop their education once they have their diplomas in their hands. They think they're finished with their education, and that couldn't be further from the truth!

We should be learning and growing every day.

Do you dedicate time each day to your personal growth? When was the last time you took an online course or hired a coach? Have you thought about what skill sets you may need to go to the next level and how you are going to achieve it?

On a scale of 1 to 10, rank yourself with how well you're doing in the category of *Personal Growth*.

Every 90 Days

Every 90 days, I want you to do this exercise and rank yourself on a scale of 1 to 10 on each of the *Areas of Focus*.

Then what I want you to do is look at the numbers that are below an 8 and start asking yourself: "What do I need to do to improve my number? How can I go from my current number to an 8, 9 or a 10?"

This is a great opportunity for self-reflection as you identify the specific areas that need improvement.

If I were coaching you one-on-one, I would go through this list with you, and dive into these areas. If we were talking about your health and you identified yourself as a 7, I would want to know how you would take that number to an 8, 9 or 10. I might even challenge you to give me two or three action items you could do to improve that number over the next 90 days.

So pretend I'm there with you. What do you need to do to improve your *Areas of Focus*? What habits can you adopt that will improve your *Areas of Focus* that rank below an 8?

Take Action:

- **Rank yourself every 90 days on the Areas of Focus.**
- **Every 90 days, set your goals to improve the categories that rank below an 8.**

Chapter 3: How to Make a Vision Board that Actually Works

"The happiness of your life depends upon the quality of your thoughts."
—Marcus Aurelius

I want to share with you the #1 reason that prevents you from living a great life.

I've had the great fortune of teaching personal development all across North America. In my live seminar, I always like talking about vision and how to create the life we want.

In my seminar, I always ask the crowd: "If I gave you one million dollars, what would you do with it?"

The expressions on the attendee's faces are priceless. They'll think about it for a few seconds and then start yelling out what they would do with the money. I love hearing their answers.

Without fail, someone will always shout out, "Travel!"

And that's my cue to dive deeper.

"Where would you like to travel to?" I'll ask.

They'll look at me confused because they haven't thought past the general concept of *travel*.

They'll say, "I don't know. Just travel, I guess?"

I then jokingly respond, "Well, you traveled to my seminar. Do you feel your life is fulfilled?"

At that point, I usually get a nervous chuckle from the crowd, but the message is clear:

The #1 reason why people don't get what they want is that they don't know what they want.

I will then prod the person who said travel to give me more details on where they'd like to go.

I can always see the change in their expression because they're now starting to gain clarity. Their answers improve.

I'll now hear:

"Paris for Christmas!"
"Bora Bora for our anniversary!"
"Visit Japan in the Spring to see the Cherry Blossoms!"

Now that's much more exciting and fulfilling than just saying *travel*.

We all travel. We do it every day. But where could we travel to that will help us live a more vibrant life?

==

Life is like a menu.

It's important to create and define the life we want to live.

It's important to be proactively building the life of our dreams as opposed to being reactive to the circumstances that have been given to us.

I like to think our lives are a lot like going to a restaurant. After we sit down, we're handed a menu and we get to choose what we want to order for our meal.

Life is much like this. I believe we can pick the experiences and the life we want to create. But first we have to define what it is we are hungry for and then put in the work to achieve it.

I remember traveling to Edinburgh, Scotland with my wife. We love to travel. And I remember walking along the streets after dinner and looking up at the incredible castle on the hill.

I started to get a little emotional because I never thought growing up as a kid I would witness such beautiful historic sites that I'd read about in books.

I grew up in a small town in Indiana in the United States. It was a classic midwestern town with cornfields and basketball hoops everywhere. With that small town also came a lot of small-town thinking and widely accepted limiting beliefs.

Eventually, I broke past my small-town thinking and started living an extraordinary life.

When I was walking through the streets of Edinburgh, I felt emotional for two reasons. The first reason was gratitude that I was able to experience the beauty of Scotland. The second reason for being emotional was that I knew I had to dream bigger.

When reflecting on the moment, I soon realized it wasn't at all hard to travel to Europe. Many people say, "One day I'll go," or "Once I achieve XYZ, then I'll travel to Europe." Like them, I had limiting beliefs that I put on the experiences I wanted to create for myself.

Once I realized experiencing Europe was easier than I imagined, I started wondering, "What other limiting beliefs do I have in other areas of my life? What other glass ceilings do I need to break through?"

When my wife saw I was getting emotional during our walk through Edinburgh, she asked, "Are you okay?"

My reply to her was, "I need to dream bigger."

==

On your path to creating the life you desire, I want you to make a Vision Board. This activity is so easy to do but also easy not to do.

This exercise involves dreaming, defining and gaining clarity regarding the life you want to create.

What I want to ask you is kind of along the same lines of, "If I gave you a million dollars, what would you do with it?"

I want to go further than that...

If you had all the passive income you desired coming in every month, what would life look like then for you?

- What would your perfect day look like?
- What does your house look like?
- Where is it located?
- How many bedrooms?
- What types of cars are parked in the garage?
- What are the interior and exterior colors of the car(s)?
- Who are the people in your house?
- Are you married?
- Do you have kids?
- How many kids?
- Do you want to travel?

- Where would you travel?
- What would you do once you were there?
- Is there a charity you'd like to help?
- Would you write a big check to them every year or volunteer your time or both?

These questions can help direct our focus on what we want for ourselves.

My challenge for you is to create a Vision Board with pictures of what you want and the experiences you want to create.

The goal is to get your dreams and goals out of your head and onto a place where you can visually see them every day.

How to Create a Vision Board

There are many ways that you can create a Vision Board. Here are the top three:

1. Get a poster board and cut out relevant pictures from a magazine. Glue them to the poster board.
2. Print out pictures from the internet and frame the pictures on your wall to create a more elegant Vision Board.
3. Buy a digital picture frame and upload pictures from the internet. Then place the digital picture frame in your office or living room where you see it every day.

Personally, Option Three is my favorite. I love being able to look at my digital picture frame and see it cycling through the pictures. It's more elegant and easier to find pictures using Google than to search through magazines to find relevant ideas.

One last thing to add is that if you're married, have a partner and/or have children, get them to participate in creating a Vision Board with you.

It's a bonding experience to sit down with those that you love the most and say, "Let's create this amazing life *together*."

You'll be amazed by the things you may learn from your partner or children about what they want out of life, and in return, they may discover some new things about you, as well.

Like I said earlier, this exercise is so easy to do, and so easy not to do. Do yourself a favor—if you want to live an incredible life, make a Vision Board. You'll thank me later.

Take Action:

- **Create a Vision Board.**
- **Look at your Vision Board in the morning so you can set your day's intentions.**
- **While looking at the Vision Board, visualize the moment with your senses. Envision what it might be like to see, taste, touch, smell and feel that moment.**

- Look at your Vision Board before going to bed so that you can program your subconscious mind to go to work on your goals as you are sleeping.

Section 2:
Optimize Your Health

Chapter 4: Boost Your Energy

"The greatest wealth is health."
—Virgil

I want you to imagine a three-legged chair. When you have all three legs, the chair is stable. When you break one leg, the chair is compromised and will rarely work. Your health is also like a three-legged chair. The three legs are represented by your nutrition, exercise and sleep. All three are vital in optimizing your health.

Now, I'm not going to give you an exercise plan or a diet. I'm not a healthcare professional by any means, and I certainly don't play one on TV. Always, speak with your healthcare professionals. What I do want to do is point out a few areas and ask you where you think you could improve.

Nutrition

First, let's talk about the fuel we put into our bodies.

Imagine you were given an incredible sports car at an early age. It has all the bells and whistles. This car is worth over a million dollars! Now imagine that expensive sports car in your driveway.

That high-end car needs fuel, and you have to fill it up regularly for it to move. You have three options to choose from:

- Cheap Gas
- Midgrade Gas
- Premium

Here's the thing—cheap gas is going to make that sports car break down faster. Sure it's cheap and you'll save money in the short term, but later on, those car repair bills will be costly.

Midgrade gas will be better, and you'll have fewer problems in the future. Sure it costs a little bit more, but it's an investment over the long term.

Premium gas is exactly what the sports car craves and will help it perform at its very best even longer. You'll find sustained high performance throughout the life of the vehicle, and you may even find you increase the life expectancy of this vehicle.

Knowing you were given this expensive sports car and you wanted to keep it your whole life, what kind of fuel would you put into it? The cheap stuff or the premium gas the car craves?

I know it's a silly analogy, but that's exactly what we have with our bodies. We have this incredible vehicle that we were given at birth, and we only have one body until we die. We can nourish it with the cheap stuff and have problems along the way, or we can fuel up with quality foods that will help us perform at our best.

There have been countless books written on the subject of nutrition and diets. There seems to be a new fad diet popping up every year.

There is the Paleo Diet. Then there is the Keto Diet. You can be a vegan, a vegetarian or an all-out carnivore. I'm not here to tell you what to do with your body, but I do want you to find a plan that works best for your own individual body.

Find a plan where your body is receiving the nourishment it needs. In America, we're overfed and undernourished. Focus not just on quantity, but also on the quality of the food you choose to eat.

==

My question for you is this—on a scale of 1 to 10, how would you rank your nutrition? Give this some serious thought.

Now that you have established your number, what nutritional habits will you have to start or stop doing to get you to a 9 or 10?

What daily, weekly, and monthly habits can you start doing? Are there any books, courses or coaches that may help you

get there faster?
Exercise

Just like all the different types of diets, there are many different exercise options. Some people swear by cardio training, some swear by strength training, while others swear by both.

For me, my workout routine consists of cardio and strength training, but you have to figure out what works best for you and your body.

Personally, I'm not built like a runner. I'm more built for strength. However, I do know that cardio training is important for my health, and therefore I incorporate at least two cardio sessions a week into my routine.

However you choose to exercise, I want you to have a plan for it. If you don't have a plan, then you plan to fail. We aren't in business to fail, we are in business to succeed, so find a plan that works best for your body type.

Then, I want you to be intentional about how you exercise. I want you to take that plan and put it on your calendar. As with many things in life, if it's not on your calendar, then it doesn't exist... It's just a dream. Put your workout routine in your calendar and you'll find that you'll have a better chance for success.

For me, my exercise routine looks like this:

Sunday: Upper Body Strength Training
Monday: Lower Body Strength Training
Tuesday: H.I.I.T. Cardio Training
Wednesday: Upper Body Strength Training
Thursday: Lower Body Strength Training
Friday: H.I.I.T. Cardio Training
Saturday: Rest

This schedule is what I do for myself. Always, always, always speak to your healthcare professionals before starting any exercise program.

==

My question for you is this—on a scale of 1 to 10, where would you rank yourself in the category of exercise? Give this some serious thought.

Now that you have established your number, what exercise habits will you have to start doing to get you to a 9 or 10?

What daily, weekly, and monthly habits can you start doing? Are there any books, courses or coaches that may help you get there faster?

Sleep

Now we are at the last leg of the three-legged chair. It's one of my favorite things in the world—sleep.

Sleep is one of the most overlooked parts of our health. We take it for granted, but it is perhaps one of the most important legs of the chair.

There are many health benefits of getting a proper night's rest; however, the problem is, we have glamorized people who get little sleep and grind and hustle all day long.

Guess what happens to those people? They burn out, their stress is high and their cognitive abilities suffer as a result. Not to mention all of the long-term problems they will have down the road.

Great sleep is imperative for great brain health. I implore you in your journey of personal development to study brain health. There are many great books out there by qualified doctors explaining the benefits of sleep. I couldn't do it justice explaining the benefits of sleep while entire books are written on this singular topic.

What I will say is that the CDC recommends adults get seven-to-nine hours of sleep per night. I want you to be intentional about your sleep. I want you to focus on both the length of sleep and also the quality of sleep. I want you to wake up at the same time every day. I also want you to go to bed at the same time every night. This way, your body can get used to this pattern.

If you want to get better sleep, here are 10 Keys to great sleep:

1. Reduce blue light exposure in the evening
2. Avoid caffeine intake later in the day
3. Have a consistent bedtime routine
4. Optimize your bedroom for sleep
5. Avoid late-night meals
6. Avoid alcohol three hours before bedtime
7. Exercise during the day but not four hours before bedtime
8. Meditate or read before bed
9. Take supplements designed for better sleep
10. Block your clock to reduce the anxiety of your wake-up time

==

My question for you is this: on a scale of 1 to 10, where would you rank yourself in the category of sleep? Give this some serious thought.

Now that you have established your number, what sleep habits can you start or stop doing for you to get to a 9 or 10?

What daily, weekly, and monthly habits can you start doing? Are there any books, courses or coaches that could help you get there faster?

Take Action:

- Create daily, weekly and monthly routines for nutrition, exercise and sleep.
- Put premium fuel into your body.
- Plan your exercise routine in your calendar.
- Get seven-to-nine hours of sleep every night.

Chapter 5: How to Meditate for Beginners

"The mind is definitely something that can be transformed, and meditation is a means to transform it."

—Dalai Lama

Just a few weeks before writing this, I was in a mastermind with 23 real estate investors. These were some heavy-hitting real estate investors with an estimated $10B in assets managed. The mastermind was designed to share best practices in their business and personal lives.

If you ever get a chance to be a part of a mastermind, I'd highly recommend it. Some amazing benefits come from being a part of a group of like-minded people to help you grow and reach the next level.

One of the lessons that stood out to me was from a member of the mastermind. Now, I'm going to keep the details of this person private because what is shared in a mastermind should be kept confidential. However, I wanted to share with you a lesson he shared with the group.

I will call this person Tim. Tim is a high performer. He has multiple businesses. He is financially free. And he's in his 50's.

He shared that he doesn't look at R.O.I. (Return on Investment) as much anymore, choosing instead to study his R.O.E. (Return on Effort). Tim shared that a few years ago his blood pressure was through the roof and that he had three panic attacks that led him to a significant life change.

He described the panic attacks as the scariest thing he'd ever experienced. Each time, he thought he was having a heart attack and rushed to the emergency room, only to find that his heart was in fairly good condition. It was always diagnosed as a panic attack.

That's when he shared the secret to what turned his life around. The secret for lowering his blood pressure. The secret to him being happier. That secret was meditation.

He started a daily practice of mediation, and it gave him his life back. And so, if an uber-successful real estate investor and countless other high performers are doing it, I highly recommend you do the same, as well.

BENEFITS OF MEDITATION

I want you to imagine that there was a drug that could do these things:

1. Reduced Stress
2. Create Emotional Balance
3. Increased Focus

4. Reduced Pain
5. Reduced Anxiety
6. Increased Creativity
7. Reduced Depression
8. Increased Memory
9. Increased Compassion
10. Increased Productivity

Source: Maryland Addiction and Recovery Center

What a miracle drug to have all of those benefits! People would certainly pay top dollar for this drug. But what if I told you that this miracle drug was free—and that you could take it as much as you want?

Well, that miracle drug is meditation. It costs nothing and the benefits are exponential. So, let's get started!

How to Meditate for Beginners

There are MANY different ways to meditate and approaches to the practice of meditation. I want to encourage you to find a practice that works best for you.

Many of my clients are new to meditation. Internally, they've always wanted to try it, but they didn't want to seem like a weirdo for doing it. But let me say this—most high performers have a daily practice of meditation. Don't let the judgment of others persuade you otherwise.

The first thing that I want you to do is to carve out ten minutes out of your day so you can be free from distractions. Find a quiet area where the kids or pets won't disturb you.

This may be in another room. It may be in your car. Just find a place where it's peaceful and you feel safe to close your eyes without being bothered.

Next, I want you to relax. If you can sit down, I encourage you to sit in the Lotus position. That is basically where you are sitting crossed-legged. If you are in your car, then that's fine, as well. Just get in a comfortable seated position.

I want you to set a timer for 10 minutes. This is how long you will be meditating. Later on, you can increase your practice to 20, 30 or even 60 minutes, but for now, just focus on 10 minutes.

Setting a timer for 10 minutes allows you to be more in the zone of meditation and not worried about looking at the clock. When you are constantly looking at the clock trying to figure out if your 10 minutes are up, that thinking will derail you from your meditation goals.

Okay, so you are now seated in a comfortable position, and you've set your timer for 10 minutes. I want you to close your eyes and focus on your breath. Breathe in slowly. Hold it for a few moments, and then let it out slowly. Focus on the pattern of your breath.

The idea is to clear your mind of all that is going on in your head. Often our brains are like a computer with too many programs running in the background. When you have too many programs running, it bogs down the performance of the computer and slows everything down. It doesn't run at its peak state. And just like a computer, our minds are very similar. Every so often we have to close down the programs and restart our computers. Meditation shuts down some of the programs running in the background of our minds and allows us to come back with greater mental performance.

So back to the moment…

We are seated comfortably, the timer is set, our eyes are closed, and we are focused on our breath. At this point, we may have random thoughts pop into our heads. We may feel as if we left the stove on and we have to go and check it. When you feel your thoughts drifting away from you, bring them back to your breath. Breathe in, hold, and breathe out. Repeat this over and over again until you hear your timer go off. And then go about your day as normal.

My suggestion is to do this twice a day. Do this once in the morning and once in the evening. You may be surprised to discover so much more joy and happiness when you have a daily practice of meditating.

Personally, I feel my cognitive abilities are even better when I meditate.

You may even find that when you first start doing ten minutes, it will feel like the longest ten minutes of your life, but with time you'll be craving more meditation time. When you feel like ten minutes isn't long enough, then I'd encourage you to increase it to fifteen minutes, and then twenty minutes, and so on.

My challenge to you is to practice ten minutes of mediation tonight. Do it before you go to bed, and you'll find more peace of mind before you lie down to sleep.

Take Action:

- **Add mediation to your morning routine.**
- **Add mediation to your nightly ritual.**

Chapter 6: Selfcare is NOT Selfish

*"An empty lantern provides no light,
self-care is the fuel that allows your
light to shine brightly."*
—Author Unknown

I want to let you in on a little yet large secret of high performers. They are very intentional about how they recover. Recovery is the key to getting ahead.

Think about how we build our muscles when we lift weights. When we lift heavy weights, it creates stress on our muscles, and that stress causes microtears in the fibers of our muscles. Our body then repairs itself with protein and grows back bigger and stronger.

When we properly rest our muscles, that's where we see our biggest gains. However, if we overload and stress our muscles too much or too often, that's when injuries can occur.

Just like our muscles, an appropriate amount of stress is key to our personal growth. Too much stress can cause damage, and not enough stress will keep us from growing into our potential.

The important part is being intentional about how we recover on a daily, weekly, and monthly basis. When we are reactive to our stress, it is often too late, and we may experience burnout.

I want to give you three areas of your life to think about where you can be intentional, not reactive, in your path to self-care. We are going to talk about the body, the mind, and the spirit and give you some examples of how you can care for yourself in each area.

The Body

First, let's talk about our physical bodies. The science behind the human body ceases to amaze me. Every day, we put a lot of stress on our bodies. Many people have poor posture as a result of sitting in front of a computer all day. Our eyes are strained from constantly staring at screens. We aren't as active as we should be. And we are overly caffeinated, just to name a few common problems.

With all the stress we put ourselves through, I want to give you my five favorite ways to help care for our bodies.

1. *Cold Therapy*

There are many benefits of cold therapy. Studies have shown it to decrease inflammation, improve your mood, increase your metabolism, recover faster from workouts and even boost your immune system.

My favorite way to use cold therapy is cryotherapy, which I do at least once a week. It can get expensive, so there are other, cheaper ways you can tap into cold therapy—ice baths are great, and even a cold shower can help, too.

2. Heat Therapy

The benefits of heat therapy are caused by improving the circulation of the blood because of the increase in temperature. This helps with muscle recovery and improves mobility in our range of motion. And it's also been shown to help with decreasing inflammation, as well.

My favorite heat therapy is infrared saunas. I like to spend 30-45 minutes in an infrared sauna while doing yoga. I'm able to increase the stretches in my yoga poses while sweating out the toxins. I feel like a new man when I'm finished.

3. Massage

I don't think I really need to explain all of the benefits of a massage, but this should be on your list of recovery items. Personally, I have a biweekly massage on my calendar.

My muscles feel better, and my mind always goes into a meditative state while getting a massage. I feel so much happier and at peace after walking out of a massage.

4.   Chiropractor

Here is another biweekly recovery session in my practice, which I do on the weeks I'm not getting a massage.

I believe we not only need to help our muscular system through hot therapy, cold therapy, and massage, but we also need to be intentional about the recovery of our skeletal system.

Our bones often get out of place from poor posture or even traumatic events like sports injuries or car accidents. Getting a chiropractic adjustment can work wonders on your overall health.

5.   Stretching

As we get older, our mobility appears to deteriorate, and we get stiffer and stiffer.

I'm a huge proponent of stretching, especially in the morning. When we wake up, our bodies have been in one place for the last seven-to-eight hours, and they are naturally stiff. I like to do 10-20 minutes of yoga to help open up my body.

The interesting thing is that most people will get out of bed stiff and go to work stiff. That stiffness follows them around throughout the day—not just physically, but in how they express themselves to others. Because they are stiff, so are their expressions. When you open up your body through stretching, you'll also find that you express yourself more openly, as well.

The Mind

Next, let's focus on taking care of our mental health. I'm proud to say that we've made some great strides in improving our mental health in recent years, but we still have a way to go. Here are five areas I recommend for improving your mental health.

1. Read a Good Book

Feeding your mind with a good book can be great nutrition for the mind. With all the negativity in the world pressing down upon us, we have to be intentional about feeding it with positivity.

Reading has been shown to improve brain connectivity, reduce stress and prevent cognitive decline, just to name a few benefits. So great job on reading this book! I want to celebrate you for making the effort to improve and recover all at the same time!

2. Time with Friends

Take time to go out to dinner or even visit a coffee shop with a friend. Catching up on each other's lives can add a little extra vibrancy to your life.

Humans have an innate desire for connection, and with how busy we can get, it's easy to put off our friends. I'd like to challenge you to make a connection with your friends every week.

3. *Celebrate Your Wins*

I am a huge proponent of celebrating your wins, big or small. When we celebrate our wins with a nice dinner or buy a little gift for ourselves, we start creating positive momentum in our lives.

I once bought a watch in January after having an amazing year the previous year. That watch was a great reminder on my wrist of my past successes and helped me remember I could have more successes in the future.

If you're buying something, don't break the bank. Going out and rewarding yourself with a little shopping can put a pep in your step. You can even reward your wins with ice cream or something small. The bottom line is just to figure out a way to celebrate your achievements.

4. *Watch a Good Movie*

I'm not a fan of watching TV. There's too much negative news on TV, but now and then, I like to watch a movie that will help inspire me. Sometimes we get in such a mental fog that it's important to get out of our own heads and plant ourselves into another story.

Find yourself a positive movie or a comedy that will help bring you out of the fog.

5.   Listen to Uplifting Music

This can easily be implemented daily. All the stresses of our life can weigh down on our mental bandwidth. We tend to entertain all the tasks and to-do's in our head, and it may overwhelm us.

Your favorite positive music can help get you in the zone or relax you, depending on what's needed in your life at the moment.

The Soul

Last but not least, let's talk about the soul and some self-care practices. I'm not going to take a religious tone to this area, but you are certainly welcome to do so if you like. I'm going to give you five practices to help your soulful recovery.

1.   Mediation and/or Prayer

I highly recommend creating a daily practice of meditation. Meditation has so many health benefits, but I'm just going to tell you that I feel mentally sharper and less stressed when I consistently practice meditation.

2.   Sleep

Getting seven-to-nine hours of sleep each night will work wonders for you physically, mentally and spiritually. Sleep is usually one of the biggest sacrifices busy people make, but the reality is that we need to prioritize sleep. Sleep is a NEED and not a WANT.

3.   Vacation

Being intentional about taking time out of your day-to-day grind is important for self-care. Exploring a new city or country is exciting and invigorating. It causes a nice dopamine release while experiencing something new, such as a new culture or art exhibit.

Take time for yourself to go out and explore. You can even do a staycation and visit something in your town that you've been putting off for a while.

4.   Journaling

I recommend this as a daily practice. There are many paths to journaling in regard to what to write. You can create a timeline of what you did during the day. You can write down what you're feeling or what you're striving to accomplish. It's great to get the thoughts out of your head and onto paper.

If you are struggling with stress and anxiety, write down all the things that are stressing you out at the moment. In your head, you may feel as if there are a million things that are stressing you out, but when you list them on paper, you'll discover that there are only maybe three or four things truly causing the stress. It feels more manageable when we itemize the root causes of our stress.

5.   *Get Out into Nature*

Taking a walk outside and into nature can be great for the soul. As a society, we are constantly indoors and out of the sun. The problem with many of us is that we lack Vitamin D from the sun that may make you very happy.

Getting outdoors not only helps us to soak in a little sunshine, but it also helps us smell the fresh air, hear the birds chirping and ground ourselves in nature. It's a humbling experience, and I always go home a happier man from being out in nature.

==

I'd like to challenge you to start adding some of these self-care practices to your calendar. If it isn't in your calendar, then it typically won't happen. Being proactive in self-care is vital to staying on top of your game.

I'd like to challenge you to create at least one *daily* self-care routine. For me, that is mediation.

I'd like to challenge you to create at least one *weekly* self-care routine. For me, that tends to be hiking in nature on Sundays.

I'd also like to challenge you to create at least one *monthly* self-care routine. For me, that tends to be a road trip to a new city or a vacation somewhere new.

Take Action:

- **Create daily, weekly and monthly self-care routines.**
- **Put your self-care routines in your calendar.**

Section 3:
Simple Ways to Become
More Productive

Chapter 7: Create Achievable Quarterly Goals

"Setting goals is the first step in turning the invisible into the visible."
—Tony Robbins

Here is the thing about five or 10-year goals—I don't like them. They are too elusive. It's easy to procrastinate and push back projects another month or two because five or ten years are so broad in scope.

I prefer 90-day goals the most. Why is that? They are more within our grasp. They feel more tangible. They appear closer.

I think of a story told by Will Smith. "You don't set out to build a wall. You don't say, 'I'm going to build the biggest, baddest, greatest wall that's ever been built.' You don't start there. You say, 'I'm going to lay this brick as perfectly as a brick can be laid.' You do that every single day. And soon you have a wall." Just like our goals, we start brick by brick, and soon we're living an amazing life.

Life is Like a Game

I find the parallels between sports and the real world interesting. Just like the game of basketball, the year has 4 quarters. And what makes up a quarter? Ninety days is the perfect amount of time for setting and achieving your goals.

Every 90 days, I want you to go through the Areas of Focus exercise and evaluate how well you are doing. How have you progressed? Where can you make better progress? Look at your Vision Board and use that as a guide to setting your goals.

I found that the sweet spot for setting 90-day goals is between three-to-five major goals. A little later in this book, I'll share with you how to tackle your goals, calendar and to-do list, but for now I want you to focus on the bigger picture.

Again, every 90 days, I want you to set three-to-five major goals. These could be financial goals. These could be health goals. You get to choose your bricks, but I want to challenge you to have a laser focus on these goals.

Just like Will Smith said, "I'm going to lay this brick as perfectly as a brick can be laid." you are going to be doing your 90-day goals as perfectly as a 90-day goal can be accomplished.

I do want to warn you about setting vague goals. When you have vague goals, you tend to get vague results. What do

I mean by that? After I challenge someone to set a 90-day goal, often I hear them tell me something like they want to improve their health. They want to "feel" better.

That may look good at first glance, but how do you *quantify* that goal? How do you know when you've hit that goal? It's too vague. That's when I dig in deeper and ask them how they can *quantify* the goal. Then I'll get something a little better, where they'll set their desired weight or the body fat percentage they want to achieve.

Quantifying losing 20 pounds is so much easier than trying to quantify "feeling" better.

At the end of 90 days, what results do you want to see in your life?

That's my challenge to you—to set quantifiable goals. Set three-to-five major goals every 90 days.

Take Action:

- **One week before a new quarter, set three-to-five quantifiable 90-day goals.**

Chapter 8: Supercharge Your Productivity

"If you fail to plan, you are planning to fail."
—Benjamin Franklin

I've had the pleasure of coaching many people through the years—everyone from celebrities, investors, business executives and everything in between. And though their professions or life circumstances are different, what remains the same is their desire to become more focused and more productive.

I often hear what's going wrong first. I hear a lot of clients chasing after shiny objects. Some are distracted by all the emails in their inbox. For some, they just don't know how to prioritize their day. And for others, they just were never given a system to be more productive.

My goal is to help you to be more productive and focused on the things that matter most.

===

Daily To-Do Lists

First, let's start with having a to-do list EVERY single day.

Where a lot of people go wrong with to-do lists is that they have a very long to-do list. Here is what usually happens. They either:

A: See the huge list and are overwhelmed and don't do anything.

B: They do three out of ten tasks on the list, but then they feel like a failure because they neglected seven other tasks.

C: They do the ten tasks the first day, they do another ten tasks the next day, and then they are completely burnt out by the third or fourth day.

Does any of this sound familiar?

What I've found is that the magic number for getting things done is *three*. Just like the Schoolhouse Rock song, "Three is the magic number, yes it is…It's the magic number."

For most people, our brains can wrap around having three tasks a day. It's much easier to remember three tasks over 10 tasks. It's much easier to tackle three tasks over 10 tasks. However, the caveat is that these aren't just *any* tasks, but are the important tasks designed for getting results.

The first task on your list.

The first task out of the three tasks, is what I call *The Needle-mover*. This is a high-priority task. This is a task designed to help get you closer to your 90-day goals. This task should be thought of this way: "If I only did this one task today and no other tasks, my day would still be well worth it. My day would still have been productive." That's how we need to frame this *Needle-moving* task in our minds.

This *Needle-mover* should be done before any other tasks on your list. Ideally, this should be done early in the morning when your mind is fresh, and you are at your best. Mark Twain once said, "If it's your job to eat a frog, it's best to do it first thing in the morning. And If it's your job to eat two frogs, it's best to eat the biggest one first." You may not be eating frogs, but you've got some big goals and dreams, and it's important to tackle those first.

The second and third tasks on your to-do list.

The next two tasks on your to-do list are what I call *Secondary Tasks*. These tasks are medium to low priority. These are tasks that are important, but they take a backseat to the *Needle-mover*.

What type of tasks are these?

- Dry-cleaning
- Getting the oil changed in your car
- Yardwork
- Grocery shopping
- Going to the store
- Etc.…

These are tasks that need to get done, but the world isn't going to fall apart if you don't do them today. Once we get our *Needle-mover* done, then we can focus on the *Secondary Tasks*.

Side Note: There are some days you may have the bandwidth to add more *Secondary Tasks* to your list. On these days, I recommend you add two more tasks to your *Secondary Tasks* list. That will give you a total of five tasks for the entire day. But beware—if you do this too often, you'll be on the edge of burnout before you know it.

So again, the ideal sweet spot for your to-do list is having three tasks. One *Needle-mover* and two *Secondary Tasks*.

Here is an example. If I were a real estate investor:

Needle-moving Task:

- Send out 100 direct mail letters to out-of-state property owners.

Secondary Tasks:

- Pick up materials from the hardware store.
- Drop off dry-cleaning.

Here is an example if I were a CEO:

Needle-moving Task:

- Create five strategies to increase Gross Profit.

Secondary Tasks:

- Attend marketing meeting.
- Email back CFO on his budget proposal.

Here is an example if I were an Actor or Actress:

Needle-moving Task:

- Memorize the script for tomorrow's scene.

Secondary Tasks:

- Send Sally flowers.
- Get the car washed.

==

Sunday Planning | Part 1: Your Calendar

Now, let's talk about your calendar. Everyone knows that when done right, time blocking is extremely effective. The problem is that most people struggle to time block. I just don't think they were taught how to do it properly, so I'm going to give you my system for using a calendar, and then we'll tie it in at the end with your to-do list.

First, I want you to create a habit of spending 60-90 minutes every week planning your upcoming week. I am a fan of either doing it Sunday morning or Sunday evening. Your first time block is to block off 60-90 minutes on Sunday and have that as a recurring event on your calendar.

Next, what I want you to do is a brain dump onto your calendar of all of your upcoming meetings, appointments and obligations. I want you to put EVERYTHING you plan on doing next week onto the calendar.

This includes:

- Work
- Doctor's Appointments
- Gym
- Flights
- Soccer Practice
- Etc.

Also, please don't forget to plan your travel time to and from these events. A lot of our day is eaten up by travel, and many people overlook this factor.

Once we have outlined our entire week and we have it on the calendar, we now can see how busy our week is going to be. It almost creates a heatmap of each day, and we can see how the flow of the week is going to go for us.

We may now be able to see that the beginning of the week is really busy while we have other days that are a little lighter with our obligations.

Now, it's time to go to work on our to-do list.

Sunday Planning | Part 2: Your To-Do List

After we brain dump on our calendar in our Sunday Planning Session, we need to start proactively thinking about what we want to accomplish. What are going to be the *Needle-movers* that get us closer to our 90-Day Goals? What are the *Secondary Tasks* we need to accomplish? That's the second part of our Sunday Planning Session.

Knowing there are seven days per week and that we're going to be doing one *Needle-mover* per day, we need to think of seven *Needle-movers* we can accomplish for the week. Remember—these are High Priority tasks.

Next, we need to think of all the *Secondary Tasks* we need to accomplish during this week. Again, seven days per week with two *Secondary Tasks* per day equates to fourteen *Secondary Tasks*. Remember, these are medium-to-low priority tasks such as picking up the dry-cleaning or taking the dog to get groomed.

You should now have seven *Needle-movers* and fourteen *Secondary Tasks* written down.

Sunday Planning | Part 3: Interconnecting the Calendar and To-Do List

At this point, we have our entire week's calendar completed. We also have our *Needle-movers* and *Secondary Tasks* written down. But now we need to start peppering our To-Do List with how busy (or not busy) the week may be.

First, I want you to look at the *Needle-movers* and look at each task there. Assign to each task how much time you think it may take to accomplish each *Needle-mover*. You may say, "Well, this *Needle-mover* is going to take me one hour to complete. And the next *Needle-mover* will only take me 30 minutes to complete. However, a third *Needle-mover* is going to take me three hours to complete."

Now, what I want you to do is assign one *Needle-mover* to each day of the week. If Monday is extremely busy, then try to assign to that day a *Needle-mover* that requires less time. If Tuesday is a little more open, try placing a more time-

74

consuming *Needle-mover* on that day. Again, I want you to place one *Needle-mover* on each day.

Once you have all seven Needle-movers in place, it's time to assign your *Secondary Tasks* to each day of the week. Using the same process, start sprinkling the *Secondary Tasks* onto your week's agenda. Each day should now have one *Needle-mover* and two *Secondary Tasks*.

By the end of this Sunday Planning Session, you should have completed your calendar and also have a plan going into the week for all the stuff that you want to get done. You are now officially being proactive and not reactive. Congratulations!

==

The Hidden Benefits of Sunday Planning

Now, looking at this system, planning your calendar, and knocking out three to-do's per day, do you think you will be more productive? I almost always get a resounding, "Yes!"

Imagine you work this plan. You'll be getting around 21 tasks done for the week. If you do that week after week, you'll be a productivity master!

However, one of my favorite benefits of keeping this system is that it allows me to be more present with my loved ones. How does that apply? Well, think about all the times you've been at home with your family and you've got work looming over your head. You've got things swirling around in your mind, and it creates stress. You find yourself not completely engaged at dinner or playing with your kid because you're worried about all the things you have to do.

Now imagine you followed my productivity system. You worked your plan, and you knocked out your three tasks for the day. When dinnertime comes and you are sitting with the people you love, you can now be more in the moment because you aren't worrying about work. You've already knocked out your work for the day. You don't have to worry about tomorrow's work because it's already been outlined in your Sunday Planning Session. So you now can be completely in the moment and enjoy those around you and your favorite pastimes.

When you work this plan, you are planning to be incredibly productive.

Take Action:

- **Start this week by blocking off 60-90 minutes for your Sunday Planning Session.**
- **Put every upcoming event and obligation on your calendar.**
- **Create one *Needle-moving* task per day.**
- **Create two *Secondary Tasks* per day.**

Chapter 9: Win Your Day by Winning Your Morning

"When you arise in the morning,
think of what a precious privilege it is to be alive,
to breathe, to think, to enjoy, to love."
—Marcus Aurelius

One of the reasons I believe people love sports is because there are many parallels with the real world. I want to take that same approach as we discuss our morning routines and why they are so important. Many of the top athletes in the world have a certain routine as they approach the game.

Imagine a professional golfer—they square up to the ball the same way every time. They take deliberate steps, position their hips, look forward, take their eyes back to the ball and smack it off the tee. Same way every time.

Imagine an NFL kicker. Same thing. They find where the ball is going to be. Step back a few paces. Step a pace or two to the left. Give a nod to the holder and kick the ball as hard as they can. Same way every time.

Imagine a professional bull rider. They get on the bull. They put their left hand under the knotted rope. They put their right hand in the air. They give a nod, and then they take off for a crazy eight-second ride. Same way every time. (Hopefully)

Why do I bring up these examples? Because when we have specialized routines, they help us perform at our best. They allow us to tap into *High Performance.*

If you imagine any of these example athletes changing up their routines, it would be catastrophic to their performance. Imagine the golfer just walks up differently every time, or the NFL kicker switches legs, or the bull rider ties a different knot—what do you think will happen? It'll be a different result every time and probably not a very good one.

That same approach applies to our morning routines.

I believe that for you to win your day, you first have to win your morning. It's the consistent approach to your morning that will give you incredible results that will carry on throughout the day.

However, if you want to win your morning, you'll also need to win your night.

Win Your Night

Let's first start with what time you want to wake up and how much time you need to sleep. The CDC recommends that you get at least seven hours of sleep per night. I need at least eight-to-nine hours of sleep. Where is your sweet spot?

Now, what time do you want to wake up every day? Five AM? or Six AM? The choice is up to you according to your needs, but I recommend you wake up at the same time every day, even on the weekends. Yes, I know it sucks, but once you establish this rhythm, you'll be unstoppable.

So now that you've figured out what time you want to wake up, let's work backward. Let's assume you want to be an elite *High Performer* and wake up at five AM. Let's assume you need eight hours of sleep. That would mean that you will need to be asleep by nine PM.

However, if you're going to be asleep by nine PM, you just can't say, "It's 8:59 PM. I'd better hurry up and go to sleep." No—you'll have to start your winddown no later than seven PM.

Think of this time as an airplane in its landing pattern. A pilot doesn't just say, "Well, we've approached Indianapolis," and then nosedive down to the airport. Instead, about 30 minutes before landing, they slowly lower their descent and make a graceful landing on the tarmac.

Just like this approach, we need to have a graceful descent into our bed, and a part of that descent includes a nighttime routine.

Some night routines I recommend:

- No screens one hour before bed.
- No caffeine six hours before bed.
- Turning the room temperature down to 68° Fahrenheit.
- Visualizing tomorrow's agenda and the successful outcome of each event and task.
- Visualizing the things you want on your Vision Board.
- Spending time with your loved ones.
- Enjoying a good book.
- Dim your lights.
- Take a warm bath.
- Journal.

This list isn't a fully comprehensive list but do what relaxes you during the landing phase of your day. One of my coaching clients said he loves to do the dishes before bed, and it was a form of meditation for him. If that's what it takes, then I'm all for it!

Win Your Morning

Again, I recommend waking up at the same time every day. That way you'll create a rhythm to your day. Where people go wrong is they sleep in on the weekends and break the rhythm. Then it takes a few days to get back into the groove, and then before they know it, they're back to the weekend with those same bad habits of sleeping in too long.

So do yourself a favor and just keep the rhythm of waking up at the same time every single day.

Once you are up, I recommend that you have the same approach every single day, just like the athletes we spoke about earlier. It will give you a sense of grounding no matter what your day looks like or where you are in the world.

There are plenty of different morning routines out there, and I'm not going to pretend that I have the perfect solution for you. Every person is different. Every person has different needs. Every person has a different schedule. However, I'm going to give you my *Win the Morning Routine*, and you are welcome to adopt it as your own or tweak it to fit your needs.

I'll break down the four phases of my morning routine. Each phase is approximately 20 minutes long.

Phase 1: Rise and Shine

"Three...two...one... Launch!" This is what I say aloud to propel myself out of bed. I don't think about it or talk myself into staying any longer in those comfortable blankets. Just, "Three...two...one...Launch!"

Then I turn on the lights to wake up my circadian rhythm.

I walk over to my sink and splash cold water on my face to wake myself up.

I go into the kitchen and make a *Morning Mineral Cocktail*. This is a glass of water with a pinch of pink Himalayan sea salt and a squeeze of lemon. This important concoction helps us because we wake up in a state of dehydration. Don't go for the coffee first because that will exacerbate your dehydration. Focus first on hydration. The lemon is good for cleansing and the pink Himalayan sea salt is good for the minerals you've lost while sleeping, breathing and perspiring.

Once I've downed my *Morning Mineral Cocktail*, it's time to make my bed.

Phase 2: Move and Stretch

Our bodies tend to be stiff when we wake up since we've been lying in bed all night. We must wake up our bodies for the day.

At this point, I do 15 minutes of yoga to open up my body and help me feel limber.

Then I get my foam roller out and spend five minutes rolling out different parts of my body according to how stiff I feel.

Phase 3: Reflect and Plan

Once I've woken up my body, I spend the next 20 minutes waking up my mind a little more. I use this next 20-minute block to review my day's agenda and the tasks that I need to do. It also evolves visualizing my day and positively seeing how each interaction is going to happen in my favor.

You can also spend time in this 20-minute block journaling and/or in meditation.

Phase 4: Study and Grow

The final phase of my morning routine is about feeding my mind. This is a great time to read, listen to podcasts or take an online course.

I love ending my routine with nourishment for my mind. It often gives me inspiration for my day or the projects I'm working on. This 20 minutes is time well spent.

Remember...

When you win your morning, you win your day.

When you win your day, you win your week.

When you win your week, you win your month.

When you win your month, you win your year.

When you win your year, you win your life.

Win your morning...win your life!

Take Action:

- **Create a night routine that helps you to wind down.**
- **Wake up at the same time every day.**
- **Use a Morning Routine every single day.**

Section 4:
Be More Confident in Yourself

Chapter 10: How to Overcome Fear

"Being aware of your fear is smart.
Overcoming it is the mark of a successful person."
—Seth Godin

Everyone fears something.

Let me repeat that. Everyone…fears something. It's a natural emotion, and we should not hide from that. However, what we do with that fear is what separates us from success or failure.

I'm often asked how I overcome fear. The simplistic approach I use is education and action.

Let me explain.

What is fear? It's usually just the fear of the unknown. We fear what we do not know. That's the most simplistic version I can give you.

How do you overcome the fear of the unknown? It's through education. The more we educate ourselves about a certain topic, the more our confidence goes up and our fears go down.

87

Then there is action. We have to act on the education we've received. That is a huge key to success right there. It's taking big, bold, massive action.

I have a problem with the phrase, *knowledge is power*. Knowledge is not power. *Applied* knowledge is power. If *knowledge is power*, librarians would be the biggest dictators in the world, but luckily for us, they are not.

It's the people who take the time to educate themselves and *then* apply what they know who have the greatest success in life.

So let's educate ourselves on the 10 most common types of fears human beings experience and then find an action that can help us to overcome those fears.

The Fear of Being Lonely

Many people are afraid to be alone. They will stay in a bad relationship, or they will be obsessively stuck on their social media. They want to feel connected with someone, and this connection is a human need we all desire. However, the idea that we are on our own may be intimidating to some.

What actions can I use to overcome this fear?

Surround yourself with people who will help lift you up. It's been said that you are the average of the five people with whom you surround yourself. So please make sure you are intentional about the relationships you are building and with whom you surround yourself. If there is a toxic person in your social circle, get rid of him or her. It may hurt, but that's massive action. You have to get rid of the toxicity in your life. They can still be your friends but at a distance.

Also, your friend count on social media is a vanity number. Don't count that everyone on your friend list on social media will be at your funeral. I know it's a morbid thought, but with that frame of mind, I challenge you to cultivate real relationships with those you know will be at your funeral.

The Fear of Change

Mark Twain once said, "The only person who likes change is a baby with a wet diaper." Change can be scary. Our world is constantly evolving, and it can feel tough to keep up with the times. Sometimes the change we're scared of is the change we want for ourselves. Sometimes it's giving up that drink or an addiction.

If we aren't careful and let the fear of change overpower us, it can lead us to stay stuck wherever we are in life.

What actions can I use to overcome this fear?

Remember this process for growth:

"Change brings resistance, and persistence through resistance brings growth."

There is a process and flow to it every time. I'll give you an example of how when you take that action to change, eventually you'll experience some type of resistance. Let's say that the change is to lose 20 pounds. Eventually, you're going to experience some resistance. You may have some friends going out for a drink or two, and you know that if you go, you're going to have the nachos and a few cocktails, and your meal plan is going to be out the window for the night. So you have two options— you can either stick with your plan and push through the resistance and not go or you can give in to the resistance and revert to old habits.

If you push through the resistance and have the persistence to stick with your plan, you'll be closer to your goals. Sticking to your plans and pushing through resistance is where the growth happens. If you succumb to the resistance and revert to your old ways, then no growth occurs.

When you are making a change, just remember the process. Resistance will always come, but when you see resistance happening, just remember it's part of the process and keep pushing through. Keep sticking to the plan. The growth will come!

The Fear of Failure

I see this in a lot of my clients who were "perfect" students. They had great grades which may have made them successful in the academic world, but in the real world, it may create a negative effect.

Let me explain.

Because they are so programmed for perfection, they rarely take risks. They play it safe. Actually, they play it too safe. And because they limit taking risks, they limit the rewards they may have achieved from taking that risk.

Life is a constant measure of risk and reward. No risk, no reward.

What actions can I use to overcome this fear?

Act despite the fear.

Two things will happen—you will either succeed from the risk you take or you'll learn from the failure. And guess what? The best lessons and the best growth comes from failure.

If you were a professional baseball player and you hit the ball four out of 10 times, you would have a hall of fame career. That means you failed 60% of the time yet were still one of the greatest.

Michael Jordan once said, "I've missed more than 9,000 shots in my career. I've lost almost 300 games. Twenty-six times, I've been trusted to take the game-winning shot and missed. I've failed over and over and over again in my life. And that is why I succeed."

My recommendation is to take massive action. You'll either win from your actions or learn from your failures. The next time you go to make another decision, you'll be even better prepared. You'll have more knowledge. And the next risk that you take, you'll have more experience to apply to the situation.

The Fear of Rejection

"What if they say no? What if they turn me down?" Does this sound familiar?

Many people are afraid of selling. Many people are afraid of asking for a date. Many people are afraid of putting their big ideas out there because they're afraid of people who may be critical of their ideas.

It can be hard to be vulnerable. It may be hard to share your ideas. Many people will bottle up their thoughts and feelings over the fear of rejection.

What actions can I use to overcome this fear?

Rejection hurts, but it happens. It's a numbers game. You're going to get rejected, but the more *no's* you get, the more *yeses* are going to happen in your life.

We can't avoid being rejected, but we can control our emotional response to being rejected. The world will keep spinning, the sun will come up tomorrow, and we will keep pushing forward.

If you do get rejected, look for the lesson in it. How can you improve on what you did? If this situation happens again, what will you do differently?

The Fear of Uncertainty

There is a phrase, "The devil you know is better than the devil you don't know." People are willing to accept the crappy situations around them over taking a risk and experiencing a potentially better result.

They let the fear of uncertainty keep them in a holding pattern in life.

What actions can I use to overcome this fear?

Take a *calculated* risk.

Get your paper and pen out and dream up 10 different scenarios that could happen as a result of taking the risk.

More than likely, it will be a stretch to come up with 10 different scenarios, and maybe only three or four may potentially happen.

When you visualize all these different scenarios, it may help take away the feeling of uncertainty, and you can strategize the next action to take after one of those scenarios comes to fruition.

It's like being a chess master with your life. You are strategizing for two or three moves at a time. When you strategize like that, it will take the uncertainty out of your life, and you can develop a plan for achieving your goals.

The Fear of Being Judged

We all want people to like us. We want to be accepted by those around us. This is a natural feeling for everyone, but sometimes we let the fear of being judged by others affect what actions we take or do not take.

There is a funny story from Aesop's Fables that will help illustrate this point.

"An old man, a boy, and a donkey were going to town. The boy rode on the donkey and the old man walked. As they went along, they passed some people who remarked it was a shame the old man was walking, and the boy was riding. The man and boy thought maybe the critics were right, so they changed positions.

94

Later, they passed some people who remarked, "What a shame. He makes that little boy walk." They then decided they both would walk!

Soon they passed some more people who thought they were stupid to walk when they had a decent donkey to ride. So, they both rode the donkey.

Next, they passed some people who shamed them by saying how awful it was to put such a load on a poor donkey. The boy and man said they were probably right, so they decided to carry the donkey. As they crossed the bridge, they lost their grip on the animal and he fell into the river and drowned.

The thing is, if you try to please everyone, you may as well... Kiss your ass goodbye."

What actions can I use to overcome this fear?

You're going to be judged. It's as simple as that. For me, I like to channel my inner Robert Downey Jr. I love what he said: "Listen, smile, agree, and then do whatever the f*ck you were going to do anyway."

If you have a plan, work the plan. Don't let the judgments of others hinder your progress.

Work YOUR plan.

The Fear of Inadequacy

A fear that often keeps people from moving forward is their own inner belief that they aren't good enough, they don't have the talent, or they just don't quite measure up to the task at hand.

These little negative beliefs that we aren't good enough can easily creep into our minds and may hinder us from stepping out of our comfort zones.

What actions can I use to overcome this fear?

Rutherford B. Hayes once said, "Every expert once began as an amateur." We aren't going to be perfect right out of the gate. Inventions aren't perfect on the first try. Sports stars aren't perfect the first time they step into the game. It's a process that takes time, and that process will lead to improvement.

To become an expert, they say we need to have 10,000 hours in our chosen field. My mindset is that the sooner you jump into whatever you're trying to accomplish, you're starting the clock toward becoming an expert. Sure, you won't be perfect the first go around, but you'll get better with every passing minute. You just have to start!

The Fear of Getting Hurt

What if I break my leg? What if I tell her that I love her, and she leaves me for someone else? The fear of getting hurt can be applied physically or emotionally and sometimes they may be valid concerns.

The fear of getting hurt often leads to inaction. And inaction keeps us stagnant in our lives.

What actions can I use to overcome this fear?

Analyzing risk to reward is key here. For example, let's say I'm going to jump out of an airplane and go skydiving. Yes, there's a valid fear that the parachute won't open, and I might fall to my death. Has it happened? Yes. Does it happen the majority of the time? No.

When I went skydiving, I thought of the risks. I also looked at the statistics, which were far more favorable in the column of safety. In my mind, I was more likely to be in a car accident on the way to skydiving than I was to get hurt from jumping out of a plane.

I weighed the risk and reward, and the reward was justified. And then I jumped out of a plane at 13,000 feet.

Yes, I could get hurt. That was an option. However, the odds were in my favor of having an incredible moment floating over the earth. I accepted those odds and took action.

The same thing is true for you. It's important to weigh what can go right and what can go wrong physically or emotionally and then take action *if* you see fit.

The Fear of Missing Out

You've probably heard of the phrase *FOMO*. This is the fear of missing out. It's that fear there's something else better going on elsewhere, or something better than you currently have.

Marketers play deeply on this human emotion. And that's the thing about emotion—it's just an emotion. Those who can control your emotions, control you. As a side note, that's why I don't watch the news—because they play too much on our emotions and therefore control our thinking.

What actions can I use to overcome this fear?

We have to be in control of our emotions. One way of overcoming the fear of missing out is with gratitude. Being grateful for the things we have can bring us contentment and joy. Be grateful for the moment you're in. Be present with those around you. These suggestions can ward off FOMO. Having gratitude for the material items you have may also ward off FOMO from the marketers who are attempting to manipulate your emotions.

Practicing an attitude of gratitude can help in overcoming the fear of missing out.

The Fear of Losing Control

I see this fear a lot in entrepreneurs. They have a hard time growing their business because they have to relinquish some control over certain tasks. Handing over tasks or projects can be daunting because in many people's eyes, they are the only person in the world who can handle that one task. I know it sounds silly, but I see it time and time again.

What actions can I use to overcome this fear?

If you want to grow, you have to be comfortable with relinquishing some of your control.

For entrepreneurs, instead of asking themselves **How** *do I do this better?* you should be asking yourself **Who** *can do this task better than me?*

When we delegate our tasks to competent professionals, it frees up our bandwidth so we can focus on higher priorities. We should be constantly trying to "fire" ourselves from our repetitive tasks by creating systems and processes to help us focus more and more on high-priority projects.

Take Action:

- **Pick books, courses and seminars to help educate you on things you don't know.**
- **Apply your knowledge with massive action!**

Chapter 11: Daily Affirmations for Success and Happiness

"Know, first, who you are, and then adorn yourself accordingly."
—Epictetus

The way we talk to ourselves can either set us up for failure or set us up for success. The tricky thing about our self-talk is that it is very sneaky. Sometimes it's easy for doubt, fear and insecurity to creep into our thinking, and we tend to entertain those negative conversations in our minds way too long without realizing how we are sabotaging our success.

Anyone who is trying to achieve high performance will eventually have to push themselves beyond their comfort zones. When you step out of your comfort zone, you are going to be faced with challenges. It's in those challenges where we can choose to grow or to revert to our old selves.

As we step outside of our comfort zones, if we aren't careful, we'll start saying phrases like these:

"I am not good at public speaking."

"I am not a very organized person.

"I am not good at sales."

"I am not good at networking."

"I am not good at eating healthy."

And guess what?! We start programming ourselves to *not* be good at those things! Our thoughts become a self-fulfilling prophecy.

In my high performance coaching sessions with clients, I listen closely to *how* my clients speak about themselves, and when I hear these negative beliefs sneak out of their mouths, it's my job to shine a light on their limiting beliefs. I'll often have them rephrase their sentences to reflect a more positive tone.

Where their beliefs about themselves are generally exposed is when they speak a phrase that starts with, "I am." This is one of the most powerful phrases in our language. It's a statement that defines us for good or for bad, and as your coach, I want to challenge you to be more self-aware of the words you use, especially when you start a sentence with "I am."

==

How can we turn things around and use "I am" statements to tap into high performance?

My answer to that question is for you to take the time to sit down and thoughtfully write out 30 "I am" statements about yourself in the present tense.

Where people go wrong in their "I am" statements is they may say something such as, "I am a future millionaire," or "I am going to be healthy one day."

The problem with these statements is that you're programming yourself to have what you desire in some future date. The future is always out of our grasp. We'll always be chasing and never accomplishing. The best way to combat this is to use present-tense phrases such as, "I am a millionaire," or "I am healthy."

You may be thinking to yourself, *but I'm not a millionaire*, or *I'm not healthy*. That's fine for now. The key is that you program yourself to believe those things and act as if they are already happening to you.

Take the time to write out your 30 "I am" phrases. Here are 30 examples of "I am" phrases you are welcome to adopt and/or change to use for yourself. Please make them your own.

1.   I am happy.
2.   I am powerful.
3.   I am whole.
4.   I am strong.
5.   I am perfect.
6.   I am confident.
7.   I am healthy.
8.   I am full of energy.
9.   I am intelligent.

10. I am wealthy.
11. I am kind.
12. I am productive.
13. I am clear about my purpose.
14. I am well-dressed.
15. I am courageous.
16. I am funny.
17. I am inspiring.
18. I am enough.
19. I am a leader.
20. I am positive.
21. I am influential.
22. I am energetic.
23. I am a powerful motivator.
24. I am an incredible public speaker.
25. I am a great father/mother.
26. I am a great husband/wife.
27. I am a great brother/sister.
28. I am a great son/daughter.
29. I am a great role model.
30. I am successful at everything I do.

(As you read these statements, can you feel your mindset get a booster shot of positivity?!)

So now that you've taken the time to write out your own "I am" statements, let's put them into action.

When it comes time for you to step out of your comfort zone, I want you to read your "I am" statements out loud and with passion and energy. The more energy you bring to reading these statements out loud, the more you will program your subconscious mind to believe these statements to be true.

So the next time you are about to deliver that big presentation, make a sales call or step out of your comfort zone, read your "I am" statements. By reading these positive declarations, you are squeezing out any negative self-talk that may otherwise creep in. You are now proactively creating your results.

Again, the key is to read them out loud with passion and energy. You might find a quiet place in your office, home or car and then go all-in while expressing your "I am" statements!

I also challenge you to begin your day with your "I am" statements during your morning routine. Then at night, right before you go to bed, I want you to go through your "I am" statements again. At night, our conscious mind shuts down, but our subconscious mind is still going. It's here at night where we can program ourselves for success.

With that being said, I want you to say with me, "I am a high performer!"

Great job! Let's keep going!

Take Action:

- Recite your "I am" statements during your morning routine.
- Recite your "I am" statements before sales calls, presentations or when you are about to step out of your comfort zone.
- Recite your "I am" statements before bed.

Chapter 12: Projecting Confidence

"Never bend your head. Always hold it high.
Look the world straight in the eye."
—Helen Keller

Imagine you're the coach of a basketball team. It's the fourth quarter, you have the ball, and the score is tied. You call a timeout so you can regroup your team and strategize the final play so you'll win the game.

You've got a play designed, but you need to figure out who is going to take the clutch shot.

You've got two players in mind.

You look throughout the huddle and see the first player. He's sitting down, and he's got a nervous look on his face. You ask him a question and he timidly responds. You immediately know this isn't the guy to take the shot.

You look at your second guy, who's standing up. He looks like he's ready to go to battle. Before you ask him the question, he already says, "Coach, give me the f*cking ball. I'm going to make this shot."

Who are you going to choose to take the game-winning shot? Obviously, you'll select the second player who is projecting more confidence.

Similarly, in real life, people want to be around and work with people who are confident in life. If we aren't careful, we may project messages other than confidence.

My goal is to help you channel your inner confidence and tell the world that you mean business.

Look Confident

When I was in my early 20s, I was at a little deli right outside of the New York Stock Exchange. While I was trying to get a quick bite to eat, next to me a business executive was getting a coaching session over lunch.

I couldn't help but listen to the conversation. One of the things that stood out to me was the coach telling the client to invest in his wardrobe.

"Think of it as an investment in yourself and your brand," he said. He went on to say, "When you look great, you feel great, and then you perform great."

Since that moment, my goal is always to be the best-dressed person in the room. The key is not to be too ostentatious, but it's to come in one level higher than the people in the room are dressed. I'm not wearing tuxedos to every place I go. I just want to be *slightly* more well-dressed than the people in the room.

Speak with Confidence

Imagine you're at dinner with someone new and they're trying to pitch you their big idea. As they're trying to explain to you their master plan, you can't hear them very well because they are mumbling. On top of that, they keep using filler words such as *like um* and *uh*.

Are you going to do business with that person? Probably not. If they aren't speaking with confidence, their idea is probably not worth investing in.

In order to project confidence while speaking, I want you to raise the volume of your voice just slightly more than you are comfortable with. Also, be very direct in your speech. Don't use filler words. Be concise with the words coming out of your mouth.

Also, pay attention to the tonality of your voice. How is your inflection? Being too high-pitched will come across as being nervous. Speaking with more bass will project increased confidence.

Express Confidence

In communication, words contribute to 7% of overall communication, and tonality contributes to 38% of overall communication. Then you have body language. Body language contributes to 55% of our communication!

Usually, you can scan a room and tell how someone's conversation is going with another person just by looking at their body language.

There are entire books written on the study of body language and how to read people. I encourage you to pick up a book on how to read body language, but for now, I want you to think about projecting confident body language.

There are several ways that you can do that. The first is your posture. Don't slouch. Stand up straight and tall. Put your hands on your hips and spread your legs a little bit. I call this the *Superman Pose*.

Imagine Superman standing straight and tall with his hands on his hips and his chest in the air. That projects confidence. You can embody that, too. When you're feeling less confident in yourself, strike that pose, and you'll immediately feel your energy shift into confidence.

Also, keep your body language open. What I mean by this is if you're sitting, open your legs a little and lean forward.

If your suit coat is buttoned, then unbutton it. If your arms are folded, then unfold them. Open up your body language. This will also project confidence.

Channeling Confidence

Beyonce has Sasha Fierce.
Kobe had Black Mamba.
David Bowie had Ziggy Stardust.
Garth Brooks has Chris Gaines.
Eminem has Slim Shady.

The list goes on and on with successful people channeling confidence from their alter-ego.

Sometimes, taking yourself out of the equation and "acting as if" you were another successful person can help you drum up the courage you need to get through a certain situation.

You can create a character yourself and act as that character, or you can channel someone successful and act as they would act in that circumstance.

For example, if you were an investor, you might channel your inner Warren Buffet. If you were a basketball player, you might channel your inner Kobe Bryant. If you were a singer, you might channel your inner Ed Sheeran.

Acting as if you are that person may help you project the confidence you need in certain situations.

Preparation

Brain Tracy once said, "Preparation is the mark of the professional." This is so true. Professionals don't just wing it. They are prepared.

When you are prepared, you feel more confident, and that feeling will show in your body language, tonality and the words you use.

When you have an important event about to happen, how can you prepare for it? How can you practice for it? Preparing and practicing will give you the confidence you need to get ahead.

Don't practice until you get it right—practice until you can't get it wrong. When you do that, you will feel incredibly confident.

Take Action:

- **Be the best-dressed person in the room.**
- **Monitor your body language, tonality and words so they project confidence.**
- **Channel your alter-ego when needed.**
- **Be the most prepared person in the room.**

Section 5:
Becoming a Better Leader

Chapter 13: Increase Your Influence at Work

"People don't care how much you know
until they know how much you care."
—Theodore Roosevelt

One word that has received a lot of bad stigma is *influence.* I believe it's a result of internet influencers. Internet influencers have garnered a lot of ill-received attention for all the shenanigans and vanity they produce.

However, influence is the key to leadership.

Leadership is the original influencer. And the difference between a lot of internet influencers and leaders is how they interact with their followers.

Internet influencers are all about *look at me and how great I am.*

Leaders are all about *look at the team, and how well **they** did.*

It's a different mindset, one of building up other people and becoming a role model to those around you.

No matter what your professional title might be, we all have influence. We may influence a couple of people or we may influence millions of people, but the fact remains that we all have influence, and influence is leadership.

==

I want to give you a systematic approach to building up your leadership for those around you. I call it the *L.E.A.D. Process*.

L.E.A.D. is an acronym that stands for:

1. Leadership Title
2. Empathize with Others
3. Achieve Results
4. Duplicate Results

Phase 1: Leadership Title

The first phase of this leadership system is *Leadership Title*. This is the start of leadership. People listen to you because of your title and that's about it. Think of this as the ground level. It's a starting point.

Imagine you are a manager and you just hired someone new into your office. You give them a project to work on. They do it because you are the boss, and you have authority.

However, they are not likely to move mountains for you at this point. They are just doing their job because you have a title, and this project is a requirement for them to stay employed. They may give you just the bare minimum of effort.

As leaders, we don't want to stay in this zone for too long.

Phase 2: Empathize with Others

If we want to gain momentum as leaders, then the next action we need to take is to build empathy with those around us. Theodore Roosevelt said it best: "People do not care how much you know until they know how much you care."

Imagine you are a manager, and you start to get to know that new hire. You sincerely ask about the person to get to know them better. You find out about their family, where they grew up and the hobbies they have outside of work. You start to find commonalities with each other.

Now imagine that you've built a sincere relationship with this new hire, and they know you genuinely care for them. Imagine you were to ask them to help you on a project. Would their work ethic be a little better? Would your influence be better? Absolutely!

Because you have built this relationship and empathized with them, your influence has dramatically increased.

Phase 3: Achieve Results

This is the next phase for leadership and building your influence. In this phase, people follow you even more because of the achievements you've accomplished.

It's about how well you produce and the results you get. You set the example of what top performers do and accomplish. People look to you as an example because you are such a high performer. They listen more intently to what you say and follow your directions without hesitation.

Example is one of the most important aspects of leadership. The better example that you set, the better your leadership will be.

Phase 4: Duplicate Results

This is where you are firing on all cylinders as a leader. This is where your influence is at an all-time high. Why? Because you are duplicating the results and successes you've achieved in Phase 3 to other people.

Imagine you start teaching and training other people to become better. Imagine you teach them how to get to the level you're currently at. Now imagine they get the results you've taught them.

How do you think they will feel about you? How strong do you think your influence will be at this point? They'll probably bust through a brick wall for you!

We should all aspire to be *Phase 4* leaders and influencers. This phase is about building up other people and giving back. This is the true essence of leadership.

Exercise:

I want you to imagine five people with whom you work on a daily or weekly basis. Which phase do you rank with them individually? With some, you may only be a *Phase 1* leader. With others, you may be a *Phase 3* leader.

Knowing which Phase you are currently in allows you to see what the next action steps are to increase your leadership.

Take Action:

- **Evaluate all your interactions with people and determine which phase you are in and what actions you need to take to level up to the next step in the L.E.A.D. Process.**

Chapter 14: A Simple Framework to Genuinely Connect with People

"Personal relationships are the fertile soil from which all advancements, all success, all achievements in real life grows."
—**Ben Stein**

When you are purposeful in becoming a better leader, you'll be required to develop deeper relationships. Many of us think we're good at building relationships, but we all have blind spots in our perspectives. Let me give you an example.

In one of my seminars, I asked the crowd to imagine they were going to take the love of their life on a very special date. I had them imagine it was their anniversary or another special occasion and they wanted to treat their significant other to a special night.

After they'd imagined the scenario in their heads, I then asked them, "How much would you spend on that special night? How much would you spend on dinner and entertainment?" I had them write down on a piece of paper the exact number they intended to spend on that date for the night.

I then went around the room and asked every person what their number was. Shockingly, almost all the numbers were different. We had the cheap people saying they'd spend about $50, and then we had others who were $500 and above along with everything in between!

It's amazing to recognize people's various perspectives, and there was no wrong answer. In their minds, they were going all-out and treating the love of their life with a special night. However, everyone's approach was different in the end.

The point is our idea of what a great night looks like is different for every person. And so it is with our relationships with those around us. We may think we have a great relationship with those we work with, but after a little prodding from me, we may discover we don't know the people around us as well as we think.

Think about a random person in your office, and let's see if you can answer these questions.

What do you know about their family? How many kids do they have? Do you know who their spouse or significant other is? Do you know what they like to do for fun outside of work? Do you know what their hobbies or pastimes are? Do you know what their aspirations are for the future? Can you tell me about their work history or where they see themselves professionally in the future?

I hope you can answer all of these questions, but if not, no worries. I'm about to give you the secret sauce for building solid relationships.

F.O.R.D.

I want to start with a framework called F.O.R.D. It's an acronym that stands for Family, Occupation, Recreation and Dreams.

Once you understand this concept, you'll know where to direct conversations. Once you understand this framework, you'll never run out of dinner conversation. Once you apply this framework, people will develop better relationships with you.

In Dale Carnegie's book *How to Win Friends and Influence People*, he famously says, "You can make more friends in two months by becoming interested in other people than you can in two years by trying to get other people interested in you."

So what's the trick to becoming interested in other people? It's understanding F.O.R.D.

Let's imagine we're at dinner with a new client. I don't know this person very well. And while most people may be nervous about what topics to talk about, we are not because of our F.O.R.D. framework.

Remember, it stands for Family, Occupation, Recreation and Dreams. I know I'm going to ask questions about each of these categories. I may spend a lot of time in one category, or I may jump around from category to category. The fact is, if I use this framework, I'll never run out of questions. And again, when we become sincerely interested in other people, that's when our relationships start to soar to new heights.

Examples of Questions

Family

How many kids do you have?
How long have you been married?
How many siblings do you have?

Occupation

How long have you worked for ABC company?
What do you like best about your job?
How did you get into this profession?

Recreation

What do you like to do for fun outside of work?
Do you have any hobbies?
What do you like to do on the weekends?

Dreams

If you could travel anywhere in the world, where would you go?
What is your dream car?
What is an experience you would love to create for your family?

Now, these are just examples, but you get the point. If you use F.O.R.D. to help guide your conversations, you'll never run out of talking points. Once someone answers a question, you can easily ask more follow-up questions to go deeper into their responses.

My challenge to you is to think about five people with whom you interact with the most today outside your own family. Think about F.O.R.D. Can you describe anything about their Family, Occupation, Recreation and Dreams?

Take Action:

- **Use F.O.R.D as a checklist when you are building your relationships both personally and professionally.**

Chapter 15: 10 Keys to Being a Great Leader

"If your actions inspire others to dream more, learn more, do more, and become more, you are a leader."
—John Quincy Adams

There are many attributes to being a great leader. This in no way is a fully comprehensive list of how to be a great leader. However, I will say, if you focus on these 10 key areas, your leadership will be ahead of the majority of the people in authority positions.

Why is that?

Well, just because someone has a title doesn't make them a leader. Just because someone has a little bit of authority doesn't make them a leader. Just because someone signs the paycheck doesn't make them a leader. Just because someone is a manager doesn't make them a leader.

True leaders are servant leaders, and servant leaders are what the world needs. We are in a leadership crisis today. More than ever, we need you to step up and be the best leader you can be. I need you to be a leader, the people around you need you to be a leader, and the world needs your example.

Here are 10 keys to being a great leader that will help jumpstart your leadership.

1. Cast Your Vision

A great leader creates a game plan on how to win. They cast the vision of what winning looks like, and they outline the steps on how to get there.

As a leader, you need to create clarity around goals and the solutions regarding how to obtain said goals. Gameplan the step-by-step course of action on achieving your goals, and then clearly and effectively outline the process to your team members.

It starts with clarity of vision and then communicating effectively, "This is how we will win."

2. Be a Role Model

There are three ways we teach. The first one is example. The second one is example. The third one is example.

As a leader, we're ALWAYS under the microscope. Get used to that. It's just the nature of the beast. But instead of running away from it, I want you to lean into it. Accept the fact that people are looking to you and use it as a platform for good.

3. Build Up Others

Leadership isn't about being on a pedestal and having everyone praise your name, although I think many politicians would like you to think that way.

True leadership is about being underneath the pedestal lifting up your people onto the pedestal and praising them for their hard work.

One quality of a great leader is that they constantly challenge those around them to dig down deeper and rise a little higher. They challenge them to do better and achieve greater things. That's what a great leader does on a day-to-day basis.

4. Keep a Positive Attitude

Before you achieve anything in life, you first have to believe you can accomplish it. If you have a negative attitude, you are already defeated.

Great leaders have an optimistic mindset, and they see the positive in every situation.

A positive mindset is contagious, but so is a negative mindset. Misery loves company, and if you start commiserating with your problems, you'll create negative momentum around them. If you want to start creating positive momentum, keep an attitude of gratitude.

5. Create Momentum

Momentum can be a juggernaut for success or failure. When you're winning, it's easier to get more wins. It becomes a snowball for success.

As a leader, you have to figure out how to get your people a win under their belt, even if it's a teeny tiny win. Celebrate that win. This may seem silly on the outside, but inwardly, it's going to spark the beginning pattern of wins.

Then figure out how to get that second win, and celebrate that one, too. Eventually with that pattern, you're going to be creating huge momentum to some very big successes.

Remember to celebrate your wins both big and small!

6. Be a Person of Integrity

Warren Buffet once said, "It takes 20 years to build a reputation and five minutes to ruin it. If you think about that, you'll do things differently."

When you are a person of integrity and stick to your word, you'll gain trust and respect. Trust is imperative as a leader. If you're always late, that will take away from your trust. If you say a meeting will be one hour and you go over by 15 minutes, you lose trust. If you give out false promises and never act on them, you lose trust.

Be a person of integrity. Be a person of value. Stick to your word because it is your bond.

7. Communicate Clearly

As a leader, you can't beat around the bush in your communication. You need to set clear expectations for those around you. When someone on your team is falling short and you need to have a tough conversation, correct the course with sharpness but show the person an increase of care immediately afterward.

Clear communication is always imperative for creating success on your team. When you are casting your vision and saying, "This is how we will win," you need to clearly define the steps your team needs to take to get to the goal.

8. Praise in Public, Correct in Private

Give other people recognition as often as you can. Ronald Reagan had a placard on his desk with a quote from Harry Truman that read, "It is amazing what you can accomplish if you do not care who gets the credit." When you and your team succeed, give the credit to the team. When you and your team fail or fall short, take personal ownership of the shortcoming. But always, always, always praise in public.

As a leader, you will encounter times when team members royally screw up. It happens. We are all humans. And when those who you lead screw up, instead of making a public spectacle of their failures, take them to the side and have a conversation with them in private. They'll respect you more because of it and will be able to save face.

9. Listen to Listen

Are you listening to what your team is saying, or are you just waiting for the person to be done speaking so you can start talking again? Guess what? People notice this detail.

When you ask questions or team members are talking, sincerely listen to what they have to say. Don't immediately jump in or cut off their speech. Take time to think out a reply and give sincere dialogue back to them.

10. Reward for Performance

Take time to reward performance. There are two ways to reward performance. The first is intrinsic rewards and the second is external rewards.

Intrinsic rewards are acknowledging a job well done. It's praising people in public. It's mentioning someone by name on a company call. Intrinsic rewards can be the best and most motivating rewards, and they cost little to nothing to the company to give them out.

The second type of reward is an extrinsic reward. This may be giving out a new TV for a salesperson hitting a sales goal. This could be treating a team to a beach vacation. This could be taking the team members out to dinner. It's a little more costly but think of this as an investment in your people. It will come back to you with interest!

Take Action:

- **Each week, pick one leadership key and intentionally work on it. For example, this week you might work on "Listen to Listen." Go out to dinner with a friend or colleague and have a dinner where you just ask a lot of questions and listen to their answers. I'd also add to cheer them on in their endeavors, too.**

Section 6:
Successfully Influencing
Others

Chapter 16: How to Make People Like You

"Be yourself; everyone else is already taken."
— Oscar Wilde

Life is easier when we work with people who we enjoy being around. Human nature tells us that we aren't alone with this feeling. People want to work with people they know, like and trust.

Imagine you're a business owner and people are constantly knocking on your door to do business with you because they feel they know you.

Imagine being able to meet a new client, and you get them to *like* you within a few minutes.

Imagine you are constantly given job advancements because your boss *trusts* you more than everyone else.

Knowing how to build your know, like and trust factor is key in building quality relationships. The faster we can get people to know, like and trust us, the faster our success will come.

KNOW

It's funny how many times I've met someone in person for the first time, and they'll start a conversation with me as if they've known me for years. Usually, it stems from some type of online connection we share, and they immediately feel personally connected to me.

And because they feel a personal connection with me, they feel more comfortable buying my courses or participating in my coaching programs.

People want to feel a connection with people who are like them, but first they have to know you.

Let's explore three ways to increase your *KNOW* factor.

1.   *Be Authentic*

We live in a world where everyone is trying to be like everyone else. And when you are trying to be like everyone else, your true self won't manifest. You may even have other people fall in love with a facade of yourself, but how long can you sustain that?

Now imagine you have people falling in love with you because of the real you. How much more gratifying will that be? Much more!

When we are our true, authentic selves, we aren't going to please the masses. It's impossible to make everyone like us. But when we are our authentic selves, we'll connect with our tribe of people.

So share openly and honestly about who you are. It'll be better for you, your sanity and your integrity.

2. Ask Questions

Where people go wrong in conversing with other people is that they only want to talk about themselves. They may let the other person reply, but then they are just waiting for their turn again to talk more about themselves. It's a one-way conversation, and it's not going to get you very far.

How do you become interested in other people? You ask questions. You can use the F.O.R.D. framework to help guide your conversation. Remember, F.O.R.D. stands for Family, Occupation, Recreation and Dreams. This is a fantastic tool to help guide your questions.

And in return, when you ask questions about other people, other people will naturally ask questions about you…And that's your moment to shine.

3. Be Specialized and Competent

When people have back pain, they seek out a chiropractor. When people have roof problems, they seek out a roofer. When people have a toothache, well, they head to the dentist.

We all should be known for something and become very skilled in that area. I'm known as a *High Performance Coach*. If people want to be more productive, have more energy and create an incredible life, they come to me, and I get them results.

My question for you is—what are you known for or would like to be known for? And are you competent in that area? Are you highly skilled in that area? Where have you developed mastery in your life?

Steve Martin was spot on when he said, "Be so good they can't ignore you."

LIKE

Who doesn't want to be liked and accepted? We all do. Not only do we want to be liked, but we want to do business with people who are like us. We would all rather do business with people who are just like us.

Kind of a funny observation while traveling the world is that when you're in a foreign land and you meet someone from your own country, you tend to gravitate toward each other.

I remember being in the United Kingdom on a bus tour to the Scottish Highlands. The bus tour had a good mix of people from all over the world, but in the beginning everyone was strangers. But by the end of the tour, little groups had started forming. You had the American group, the German group, the South American group, and so on.

For me, we started interacting with the American group. We lived hundreds of miles apart back at home, but when we were on foreign soil, there was a kinship because we'd finally found people like us.

It's a natural feeling to want to be around people who are like us, not only while traveling but in our everyday situations.

I'm going to show you three ways to increase your *Like* factor when face to face with someone.

1. *Mirroring*

A very subtle way to get someone to like you is by mirroring the other person. You are mirroring or copying the other person's gestures, body language, the tempo of their speech and/or their attitude.

Remember, people like people who are like themselves. So when we are like them with their energy or body movements, people are naturally inclined to like us.

Here are a few examples of how to mirror another person:

If they are speaking slowly, you speak slowly.
If they are gesturing with their hands, you gesture with your hands.

If they have a tonality with a higher or lower pitch, you match your tonality to their pitch.

If their legs are crossed when sitting, you cross your legs when sitting.

If they stand, you stand.

I know—you may be thinking, "Won't people catch on?" And the answer is, "No." Well, not if you do it right. They say a tactic shown is a tactic blown. Don't share with them that you're purposely mirroring them. Ninety-nine percent of the time, people will have no clue you are mirroring them.

Give it a shot. The next time you are at dinner, practice on the person you are having dinner with. See how the conversation goes.

2. Sincere Compliment

Everyone likes a compliment, especially when it is a sincere compliment. When you are giving a compliment without sincerity, it's just flattery. Flattery won't get you very far.

When you share a sincere compliment with someone, they can tell if it's sincere or not. For every person you meet, you should make it a point to share a sincere compliment with them.

On a side note: Great job for reading this book! For you to have read this far in the book tells me you are serious about being a high performer. (Did my sincere compliment work?)

3. Smile

There are so many positive psychological benefits to smiling, but when someone smiles at you, it's hard not to smile right back.

If you want to stand out from the crowd, smile more.

When you express a smile to someone, it's saying that you like them. Again, everyone has the desire to be liked, and by smiling, you are subtly saying you like them and accept them.

And when people feel they are liked and accepted, the chances that they'll like you are greatly magnified.

As an experiment, I'd like to challenge you to smile at 10 different strangers today. What I want you to do is take stock of their reactions. If I had to guess your results, all 10 strangers will smile right back at you. And though you may never know it, you may even be the sunshine in their day that they desperately needed.

Trust

Trust is the keystone of great relationships. Without trust, your relationships won't go very far. Trust is built over time and should be intentionally crafted with those who you care about. You have to be a person of integrity 100% of the time, even when it's tough.

For those who compromise their integrity, years of trust can be instantly lost. We see that time and time again from our politicians and celebrities. It can be hard to rebound from a compromise of trust.

With that being said, I want to share with you three ways you can build up your trust factor when meeting someone new.

1.   Eye Contact

We know the eyes are the windows to the soul. When people won't look you in the eyes, it's hard to trust that person. If their eyes are darting back and forth from side-to-side, it implies that they aren't telling the truth. When people look you directly in the eyes, you'll trust them more.

One tactic for increasing your trust factor when meeting a new person is when you greet them, look into their eyes just long enough to take notice of the *color* of their eyes. This may be about four or five seconds long, but it's just enough to gain instant trust and connection with the new person. It's very subtle but very impactful.

I want to challenge you today to meet a new person and try this out. Greet them, and while shaking their hand, look them in the eyes and take notice of the color of their eyes. You'll see a connection being instantly forged!

2. Humor

If you can get people to laugh, you can get people to take down their defenses, and when you get people to take down their defenses, you can get them to start trusting you.

Humor is a great way to start a conversation, a speech or even a date. Everyone loves to laugh.

Here's the thing—not everyone is a born comedian. And we should never joke about sensitive subjects or use inappropriate humor. This will do more harm than good.

One of the easiest forms of humor is self-deprecating humor. This is where you use humor to poke fun at yourself. By poking fun at yourself, you can help ease any anxiety that might be happening when meeting someone new.

What are some examples of self-deprecating humor? A short person might make fun of their own height. A bald person might make fun of their "haircut." Someone with an accent might poke fun at their speech.

What is something you could poke fun about yourself? I'd challenge you to think of three things about which you could make fun of yourself.

3. *Positive Attitude*

A positive attitude can go a long way with people. We are constantly bombarded with negativity on the news, so when you meet someone positive it's like a breath of fresh air.

I have a friend of mine, Dean Simon, who has an incredibly positive attitude. People gravitate toward him because of the positive energy that his attitude radiates. I've seen him excel past his competition because of his work ethic coupled with his can-do attitude.

It makes me think of a time when Winston Churchill said, "Attitude is the little thing that makes a big difference."

We should never complain, whine or give excuses. Sure, we all have them, but mentioning them aloud is not going to get us very far.

When we replace complaining, whining and excuses with an attitude of gratitude, you'll see amazing things start happening in your life.

When you are meeting someone new, radiate positivity. Be a ray of sunshine. Share positive stories. Be uplifting in your conversations. That positivity will help you increase your trust factor.

Take Action:

- Be authentic.
- Be specialized.
- Ask questions about others to increase the *Like* factor.
- Create good eye contact.
- Find humor.
- Be positive.

Chapter 17: A Straightforward Formula for Persuading Others

"The most important persuasion tool that
you have in your arsenal is integrity."
—Zig Ziglar

High Performers are incredibly persuasive. Not all High Performers are in sales, but they've developed the skills of persuasion to help them further their cause. We use persuasion every day. We might use persuasion with our kids, when presenting a business idea or in getting your spouse to watch that movie you've been dying to see.

Now before I get into a simple formula for persuading others, I'd like to talk about the stigma that may surround persuasion. Even if you don't have a job in sales, learning how to persuade is vitally important. I've seen engineers have incredible ideas but because they couldn't clearly present their ideas, they were overlooked.

When using persuasion, it's also important to understand that we're persuading someone to change their beliefs or ideas about a subject and bring them mutual benefit. Where sales and persuasion get a bad name is through coercion. Coercion is different from persuasion. Coercion is a one-sided transaction, while persuasion is a two-sided, mutually-benefitting transaction.

I'll give you an example of the difference between coercion and persuasion.

Let's say you go to *Honest Bob's Used Car Dealership*. You're looking for a blue sedan for about $5,000. However, Honest Bob is aggressive and sells you a $10,000 yellow SUV. It wasn't what you wanted, but it's what Honest Bob wanted. He wanted to make a higher sale to have a higher commission. He coerced you into buying an item that only benefited himself and his pocketbook, and now you're stuck with an SUV you never wanted in the first place.

Now, let's use persuasion as an example. Let's say you have a family member who is struggling with an addiction. It's your brother, and you love him dearly. However, his addiction is affecting his health, and it's hurting the people closest to him to see what he's doing to himself.

You step up and have a serious but loving talk with him about his addiction, and you persuade him to seek help. He acts on what you asked him to do, and he goes and gets some help.

Over time, his health improves. As a result of him being healthy and happy, it also makes his family happy, too.

The act of persuasion was mutually beneficial. He, you and the rest of the family benefits from you persuading him to get help.

Persuasion is a great skill to have, and when you know how to use it with good intentions, you can take your success to another level. So let's break down a simple, one-two-three approach to persuading.

1. Prepare
2. Invite.
3. Follow-Up

1. Prepare

Before your big ask of someone, you first have to prepare them beforehand. The way we do this is through empathy, desire and emotion.

First, we *empathize* with their position. We acknowledge where they are now at and what they are going through. We might empathize with their challenges or the struggles they may be facing.

We might say, "Johnny, I understand that you're going through a difficult time. You're stressed at work and going to the bar after work is your time to unwind."

Next, we're going to talk about their *desire* for a better future. We want to appeal to what they hope and want, moving forward. This could be a job promotion, an increase in status or whatever it is they want moving forward. We acknowledge what they want.

We may say, "Johnny, I know you want to be sober. I know you want to be more present with your wife. I know you want to be a better example to your kids."

Then we're going to add emotion with a story or anecdote. We have been using stories for thousands of years to teach and pass on knowledge. Depending on the situation, we could use a quick story or a long one.

We may say, "Johnny, I remember when Dad had the same problem. He'd come home drunk every night. We never knew if he was going to be happy or angry. It just made us so uneasy. Then after Grandpa died, do you remember what happened? Dad got help and sobered up. Now he's an incredible grandfather to our kids. We don't have to worry about wondering if he's going to be a happy or angry Dad. He's always happy now."

Can you see how this method of empathy, desire and emotion can help lead to the big invite?

Now, you may not be asking someone to be sobering up like in this example, but you'd use the same format to help prepare them. First, empathize with their position, then talk about what they aspire to be or have, and then follow it up with an emotional story that emphasizes your point.

2. Invite

After we prepare, then we need to have a solid call to action. We can't beat around the bush when it comes to asking for what we want. I've noticed that as Americans, we tend to skirt around asking for what we want, while I've noticed other countries and cultures being much blunter in their approach.

We need to be clear and to the point in our call to action. Don't assume the person knows what we're alluding to. Be to the point and be direct.

For example, we may say:

- I want you to move me to Row 3, Seat A on the airplane.
- Sign right here at the dotted line on the last page.
- Will you go to the movies with me on Friday at 8 PM?

Be clear and to the point on what you want.

3. Follow-Up

You may have heard that the fortune is in the follow-up. I couldn't agree more. Once we have prepared the person and invited them to take action, then we need to have a method for following up.

Following up may be checking in on Johnny to see how his progress is coming along. It may be sending a quick note to your client. It could be a phone call to that new contact you just met.

Once you've extended your call-to-action to the person, it's important to have some accountability for what you are inviting them to do.

Putting It Together

In a persuasion situation, you won't be spending equal parts of time in these three areas. If done correctly, most of your time is in Step 1: Preparing the person for your call to action. You're going to be empathizing, talking about their desires and sharing a story to hit on the emotional button.

Next, you'll spend just a little bit of your time on the actual call-to-action. Be direct and ask for what you want.

Then you're going to follow up with them, depending on what type of follow-up is merited.

Now that you know how to persuade someone, don't overcomplicate it.

Just remember—prepare, invite and follow up.

If you want to persuade someone, take the time to think out the three steps in advance, and you'll find yourself much more effective.

Take Action:

- **Practice persuasion daily.**
- **Experiment with strangers you meet like a cashier or waiter.**
- **Think through the persuasion techniques you'll use before implementing.**

Chapter 18: Developing Your Personal Brand

"Your brand is what people say about you when you are not in the room."
—Jeff Bezos

Picture and imagine the people with whom you work on a daily or weekly basis. How would they describe you? Would they call you a hard worker or would they say you're constantly late?

Here's another fun question: If strangers were to Google you, what would they find and what do you think their impressions of you would be? Are you a family person? Are you a professional?

If they searched in Google Images would they find pictures of you passed out from a long night of partying with permanent marker written all over your face? I'm being a little facetious, but I've seen a lot of crazy pictures from people I've interviewed through the years.

I've hired many people, and I'll be the first to tell you that I Google EVERYONE I interview to get a better understanding of who the real person I'm potentially about to hire.

Whether you know it or not, you have a personal brand. You can either be intentional about how you craft your reputation, or you can haphazardly let other people craft your brand for you. For me, I want to control the narrative of who I am and how I can help others.

How about you? Would you rather be known as the person who gets results or would you rather be known as the person who is always late to meetings? I'm going to guess you would rather be known as the person who gets results. When you actively develop your personal brand, you magnify your career even further.

I'm going to give you five strategies to improve your personal brand.

1.   *Think of yourself as a business owner even if you are an employee.*

The first way to improve your personal brand is to think of yourself as your own business. To set the framework, even if you are an employee right now, think of yourself as a business owner and deliver as much value as you can to your customer (employer). As you think of yourself as your own business, it will change your paradigm of thinking and will improve the quality of your output.

The problem with most thinking is that they consider themselves employees, and that sets them back.   An

158

employee's paradigm of thinking consists of, "What can the company do for me? How can I get by with the least amount of work and still get paid?" Employers hate this. Your manager hates this. It's bad personal branding to have that mindset.

As a business owner, I'm always thinking of ways to deliver and over-deliver value to my customers. My customers are my focus. They are the soul of my business. If you think of your employer as your customer, it changes the way that you focus on your work.

I promise you as a business owner myself that if I had an employee who constantly delivered value and who put my needs first, they would make the most money, have the best schedule, and I would do what I could to help them out.

As you think of yourself as a business owner, your personal brand will be strengthened with your employer as someone who delivers value. As a result, you'll put yourself in a better position to succeed with the company.

2.   *Online Audit*

The next way to improve your brand is to do a quick online audit of yourself. Start Googling yourself. What comes up? And make sure you use other search engines too like Bing or Yahoo.

If you're not Googling yourself, I can guarantee your future employers or future clients are Googling you. If you don't like what you see, you can try and change it. A lot of your online presence is your social media posts, so please make sure you aren't posting anything that isn't appropriate. Make sure you clean up your tweets and remove risky posts.

As a business owner, I've passed up on many potential candidates because of their online presence. Their social media pictures can tell me a lot about a person. So make sure you Google yourself and clean up what you can.

3.   *Your Brand's Story*

Every brand wants to convey a precise story about who they are and how they help. For example, if you are in the personal development industry like me, I constantly eat, drink and breathe personal development. I share personal development posts. I talk about my own story and how personal development has helped me.

Now what you won't find is contradicting items to my brand's story. For example, you aren't going to find me reviewing restaurants or the latest cooking recipes. Why? Because that would be inconsistent with my brand.

So if you want to strengthen your brand, stick to your brand. If you are branding yourself as a food expert, then stick to reviewing restaurants. If you are branding yourself as a fitness coach, then stick with posts about fitness. It seems like common sense, but I've seen a lot of people send mixed messages, and all that does is confuse your brand's message.

I would like to challenge you to post online content consistent with your messaging. If you want to be perceived as an expert in your field, then start producing online content that goes along with the message. As you start posting to different platforms, it will start filling the search engines like Google with positive posts. That way, when people Google you, they'll find messaging that is on-brand.

4. Elevator Pitch

Imagine that you walked into a building and made your way into an elevator headed to the top floor. Then you noticed it was just you and one other person on the elevator. However, this just isn't any person—this person is Elon Musk and you've always dreamed of being a part of his company.

So what do you do? What do you say?

Of course, the likelihood of you being in an elevator and pitching someone is small, but the process remains the same. You're going to be in situations where you have a very short period to make a great first impression. Instead of fumbling through what to say, it's important to have something prepared.

This is where you need to come up with a quick 30-60 second overview of who you are, what you do and how you can help.

Write out this elevator pitch and practice it over and over again until it becomes second nature to tell your elevator pitch to someone you need to impress.

5. Optimize Your Online Presence

Imagine that you want to hire a plumbing company, and you were referred to two different companies by a friend. Before you make your calls, you decide to do a quick web search of the two companies to see if there are any reviews or to see if you can find any more information about their business.

What you find with the first plumbing company is that they have five stars on a couple of different review sites. You also find their website and it's filled with positive testimonials. Their website has an articles section that is very informative. Their website also lists their services and prices and outlines their guarantee for happy customers.

Then you start searching for the second plumbing company. However, you can't find anything at all about this company. It's almost as if they don't exist. You've got a phone number but that's it.

Now, which company are you going to hire? Probably the first company, the one with an online presence, solid reviews and an informative website.

Just like this example, I would encourage you to have a website. Add positive content on there. Have a blog or a podcast. Find an online platform where you can post daily, weekly or monthly.

Optimize your profiles on these online platforms to showcase your expertise. Please make sure they are optimized to be cohesive with your brand's story.

Again, as you start posting with your brand's message, you are going to fill the search engines with what you want people to see. I'd much rather have your name be associated with great online content than a picture of you passed out from a long night of drinking.

Take Action:

- **Have a Business Owner mindset.**
- **Audit your online presence.**
- **Create an elevator pitch.**
- **Optimize your online presence.**

Section 7:
Growing Forward

Chapter 19: Learn How to Learn

"You will be the same person in five years as you are today except for the people you meet and the books you read."
—Charlie Tremendous Jones

One thing that many people are surprised about is that I'm not a college graduate. I don't have one college credit to my name. However, I do have an education. In my circle of friends, they know how obsessive I am about reading, and over time, that has become my superpower.

However, it didn't start like that…

When I was younger, I had plans to go to college, but I ended up getting a job, was good at that job and started to pull in a nice income. In my youth, I determined college was out. Over time, I felt guilty about that decision not to pursue formal education and receive a degree.

Yet as I look back on it now, I realize that not going to college worked in my favor. Let me explain…

Because I didn't have a degree and I was in business, I took it upon myself to carry out my own self-education. If I didn't know how to do something or if I lacked a particular skill, I started with a book. I found it interesting that you can consume years and years of someone's life work in one book. Talk about leveraging your time through someone else's experiences!

I became obsessed with reading, and over time I gained a lot of knowledge and skill sets. This made me very valuable in business and also as a coach because I was the guy with all the answers.

Today, I'm at the point where I finish one book a week, and I've been doing that for many years now.

As I've had the opportunity to coach people over the years, I've noticed where many people have gone wrong in their personal and professional progress, or shall I say lack of progress, is that most people stop educating themselves on the day they receive their college diploma.

Unfortunately, many people believe their education stops because they are now "educated," and they have the fancy paper to prove it. The reality is that their education should continue throughout their lives until their last dying breath.

I believe this is where I gained my competitive advantage because I never received a degree, and so I always kept up the habit of learning.

There's been a lot of talk about how many books the average CEO reads versus how many the average American reads. I couldn't nail down the actual statistics on the CEOs, but I've heard it's around 50 books a year. The average American reads 12 books a year according to a Pew Research Study.

Pew Research also went on to say that 50% of American adults read four books or fewer. Also, Americans who have a college degree typically get their hands on seventeen books each year, with about 50% of them finishing seven or fewer of those books.

However, 23% of adults in the US claimed they hadn't read a book in the 12 months prior to the survey.

Whatever the statistic might be, I think it could be summed up with a quote by Harry S. Truman: "Not all readers are leaders, but all leaders are readers."

If you want more from your life, the habit of reading is an absolute must!

"HOW" To Read, Not "WHAT" to Read

In my early 20's, I started my passion for reading. And then one day, my life changed when I met a speed-reader.

I was having lunch with this gentleman, and he told me he could consume a book within an hour or two in one sitting.

I honestly didn't believe him. It took me weeks to finish a book, and this guy was telling me he could do it in a few hours. I thought he was crazy.

So I did what I always did. If I didn't know something, I bought a book. So I bought a book on speed reading. Looking back, it's funny to think I bought a book on how to read a book but that was a game changer for me!

People ask me all the time *what* books I read but rarely do I get asked *how* I read. So let me explain how I finish one book a week.

Going back to that conversation with my friend, the speed-reader, he told me the first step I needed to do was to read as fast as I could read. Just an all-out sprint at first. Don't worry about the comprehension, just read the words as quickly as I could.

He said there was a method behind that, and he relayed this analogy to me about his son. His son was an incredible runner. He was training for the Olympics. One of the exercises his son's Olympic coach had him do was get on a treadmill, and they attached a special harness to him.

Then the coach had the runner run as fast as he could. I'm not sure what the exact numbers were, but just follow me on this analogy. The young man was running about 12 mph as fast as he could. This was as fast as he thought he was capable of running.

Then the coach cranked up the speed. Now, remember, the runner was attached to a special harness, so if he fell, the harness would catch him, and he would be just fine. So the coach cranked the speed up to 15 mph, then to 18 mph, and then up to 30 mph until he finally could not keep up with the speed of the treadmill. He fell, and the harness safely caught him.

He'd run so much faster than he previously thought he was capable of achieving!

Then this is where it gets really interesting. The coach then asked him to go back to running at 12 mph on the treadmill. Guess what? The 12-mph pace now felt slow to the runner. Once he'd experienced running at a faster pace, he then increased his physical and mental ability to run faster!

The same rings true for our brain. It's just like a muscle. We can train it to do amazing things. And speedreading is certainly possible for almost anyone.

==

Just like the Olympic Coach, I'm going to use the same approach to coaching you to read faster.

The first thing I want you to do is to open up an audiobook on your phone. I want you to begin a new chapter and listen to that chapter for 60 seconds. Now press pause.

Now, what I want you to do is to do an all-out sprint, just like the treadmill.

I want you to go into the settings and increase the playback speed to 2x. That means it will read the book to you twice as fast.

I want you to press play and listen to the audiobook for 60 seconds at 2x speed. At first, it's going to sound like a chipmunk reading. This may sound a little bit crazy but trust the process and just listen for 60 seconds. Try to comprehend the book as much as possible.

All right, now that the 60 seconds are over, I want you to change the settings back to normal speed. I want you to listen to the book at normal speed for another 60 seconds.

How does it sound now at normal speed? I'll bet it feels incredibly slow! It may even sound as if it's now in slow motion. Why? Because your brain started to train itself on processing information faster.

I'd love for you to start listening to audiobooks at 2x speeds, but you may have to start working your way up to that point. You may start at 1.25x, then 1.5x, 1.75x and finally even at 2x or beyond.

The reason why I love 2x speed is that it does a couple of things. First off, if you're reading an audiobook at twice the speed, then that means it's taking you half as long to get through the book. Most nonfiction books are about three-to-six hours long. Imagine that you have a six-hour book, and you doubled the reading speed. That means it would only take you three hours to get through the book.

Then imagine you are commuting to work in your car, and you have a 30-minute commute. If you listen to an audiobook at 2x speed on your commute to work and back, that means you could finish an entire book in three or four days!!! *Boom!*

One more benefit of 2x'ing your reading speed is that you increase your comprehension of the book. Let me explain...

The human brain can process between 400 and 800 words per minute. However, the human tongue can only speak about 120-150 words per minute. There is a discrepancy between how fast we can process thought versus how fast we can speak.

This is why you hear people say, "I'd love to listen to an audiobook, but I start thinking about other things and then I have to rewind the book and start over." Have you ever felt that way?

The reason for this is that your brain can process the information much faster than you're able to speak. As a result, the brain processes the information, moves on and starts thinking about other things. That's why you drift off in thought while listening.

If we double the playback speed on our audiobooks, it causes our brains to concentrate more and prevents us from drifting away in thought.

By doubling our reading speed, we not only get through a book in half the time, but it also increases our comprehension and recollection!

At this point, you may be asking yourself about physical books. Yes, this works for physical books, too, but it takes a little bit more practice.

There are a handful of ways to speed read physical books. I want to give you a simple strategy which will sound counterintuitive, but it works... Use your finger.

When we read physical books, we may also experience the same thing with drifting off in thought. It's partly because our brains process the information faster than we can read, but it's also because our eyes micro-drift off the sentences and we have to refocus our eyes to what we are reading. This constant drifting and realigning of our focus slows us down.

The solution to the problem is to read with your finger, but before we get to that point, let's set a baseline with your reading speed.

What I want you to do is pull out a physical book, get your stopwatch out and read one page. I want you to time yourself on how long it took for you to read that page. Then I want you to count how many words were on that page and divide that number by the time. This will result in your *Words Per Minute* baseline.

Next, I want you to read another page, but this time I want you to use your pointer finger. I want you to move your finger with the sentence. Your job is to have your eyes focus on the word that your finger is pointing at. Go through one page at the pace you would normally read.

Now that you've gotten used to reading with your finger, I now want you to move your finger faster. Keep your eyes concentrated on the words at which your finger is pointing. Try to double the reading speed by moving your finger faster.

Time yourself and see what your reading speed is now with reading with your finger. You'll probably see that you can double your reading speed with physical books very quickly by just using your finger.

And just like we talked about earlier, your brain is like a muscle. The more you train your brain to read fast, the stronger and more capable it will be at speed reading.

Now that you've learned how to read faster, it should help accelerate your learning and give you the secret to how CEOs can consume 50-60 books in one year.

Imagine that you start finishing one book a week. That's 52 books a year. Over five years, that is 260 books!

Now imagine the average American reads 14 books a year. Over five years, that means they have read 70 books in total. Over those five years, you would have read 190 more books than the average American. That means you would outperform the average American over five years by over 271%! I don't know about you, but 271% sounds like a HUGE competitive advantage to me.

All those books you will have consumed will give you increased knowledge and skill sets that will help improve your personal and professional lives.

From here on out, I want to challenge you to get to the point where you 2x the speed on your audiobooks and you use your finger to 2x your physical book reading speed.

Take Action:

- **Increase your playback speed to 2x on your audiobooks.**
- **Read physical books with your finger while moving your finger faster.**

Chapter 20: Achieve Your Goals Faster

*"Without a coach, people will never
reach their maximum capabilities."*
—**Bob Nardelli, CEO of Home Depot**

A few years ago, I was talking to a good friend of mine about our birthdays. Our birthdays are just a few days apart, so we came up with the idea that to celebrate our birthday that year we would jump out of an airplane.

My friend Kyle and I started to explore our options. We found a place not too far from where we lived that offered a skydiving experience.

On our quick research of their website, we had two options from which we could choose. We could do a solo freefall, or we could do a tandem jump. A tandem jump is where an instructor is attached to your back.

Now, I'm a pretty big guy, and I really didn't like the idea of having someone harnessed onto me. I like my personal space, but I digress…

As I'm looking at these two options of solo or tandem, my pride kicks in and I tell Kyle that I want to do it solo. He agrees, as well, and a few days later we made our way to the airport where this skydiving experience was about to go down.

As we checked in at the front desk, the clerk asked us if we would rather do solo or tandem. We told him we wanted to do it solo, and then he explained the two options in better detail.

Option 1: Solo

You will have to do a five-hour ground school training that covers gear, procedures and techniques essential to a safe skydive, as well as ground practice and simulations of skydiving scenarios. When completed, you'll make your first solo jump accompanied by two AFF instructors trained to assist you through the exit, free fall and parachute deployment. Another instructor will be on the ground to guide you through landing via radio.

Option 2: Tandem

A tandem skydive is the safest, most exhilarating way to experience skydiving. You are attached via a harness to a highly trained USPA-rated instructor who handles all the details from exit to landing, so you can enjoy the adrenaline rush.

You'll watch a *brief* training video. Then you'll meet your instructor for a pre-jump briefing and get geared up. Together, you'll board the plane. As you climb to jump altitude, your instructor will go over instructions again. At

13,000 feet, the door will open, and you and your instructor will exit together into blue skies. You'll freefall at 120 mph, and at 5,000 feet, your instructor will deploy the parachute. Together, you'll soar back home.

Kyle and I met each other's gazes. We hadn't realized that jumping solo would require a 5+ hour training. We didn't have time for that, so we conceded to do *Option 2: Tandem*.

We did our brief video tutorial, put the harness on and attached ourselves to our instructor. We then walked over to this tiny little plane, and off we went!

As I looked out the window, the world kept getting smaller and smaller. I've flown over a million miles for speaking engagements throughout my life, so being in an airplane wasn't a big deal for me. However, this time as I looked out the window as we climbed in altitude, I started to get a little worried.

I knew we were going to jump out of the airplane at 13,000 feet, but as we climbed, and I looked out, I couldn't help but wonder how much more we were going to climb in altitude. Surely we were close to 13,000 ft! So I asked the instructor, "Is this 13,000 feet?" He laughed and said, "this is just 5,000 ft. We have 8,000 more feet to go!"

My stomach dropped.

Now mind you, the next time you are in a commercial airplane and you take off, the captain will announce 10,000 feet and notify you that you can turn on your electronics. I want you to look out the window at that point and then realize that jumping out of a plane, well, you have 3,000 more feet to climb.

As we reached 13,000 feet, the instructor informed me that it was time. The tiny door on the side of the plane slid open and I immediately felt the cold air rushing into the plane. It was incredibly loud.

My friend Kyle was the first to jump with his instructor. They slid out to the edge of the plane, Kyle positioned himself as instructed, and they jumped out of the plane.

When I saw them jump, I expected them to gracefully start floating down to the ground. Nope! I was wrong. When Kyle jumped out, he was like a bullet being shot out of a gun. He was out of eyesight within a fraction of a second.

This was when things started to get real!

Now it was my turn to jump out of an airplane, and my anxiety level was through the roof.

We slid up to the door, I positioned myself as instructed, and with the instructor on my back started the countdown.

"Three…two…"

And he pushed us out at two. The guy didn't even get to one!

As we started free falling, I felt as if I was going to die! I'd never experienced anything close to this sensation of falling through the air, and the wind felt as if I'd put my face into a tornado.

When I was falling, I was immediately grateful that I had this experienced skydiver with 2,000+ recorded jumps strapped to my back. All my pride and ego at having someone strapped to me was gone, and a sense of relief filled my mind.

I couldn't imagine doing my first jump out of a plane solo. In the heat of the moment, I have a feeling I would have forgotten all of my training. Again, I was so happy to have the experience with this expert strapped to my back so I could lean on his guidance and just enjoy the moment.

As I floated through the air, it became a blissful experience. My emotions went from anxiety and feeling as if I was going to die to a euphoric experience. It was such an amazing moment to fly through the air like a superhero.

Then, at 5,000 feet, the instructor deployed the parachute and we gracefully landed on the ground. It was a successful jump that I'll never forget!

Later that night, I couldn't help but reflect on each step of my skydiving experience. I found a very valuable lesson from that day: If you want to learn faster and do it safer…get a coach.

Remember, I had two options on this jump.

Option 1: Solo

It meant I would have to spend much more time on training. In this instance, at least five hours.

Then after the training, I'd jump out of the plane alone and have to rely on my knowledge, hoping it goes right. In the heat of the moment, I'm sure I would have forgotten a step or two which could have been disastrous.

Option 2: Tandem

This meant utilizing the experience of a professional skydiver while walking me through every step of the way. I was able to shorten my learning curve *dramatically*, and I could lean on his expertise to ensure I had a safe experience.

Luckily, I chose Option 2.

By choosing Option 2, we jumped out of the airplane and were on the ground eating lunch and talking about our experiences before the people in Option 1 even got off the ground.

By choosing Option 2, I got to my goal faster and safer, while everyone else going solo was just getting started.

That's the power of coaching! Speed and safety!

==

Hiring Coaches

There are many different types of coaches out there. I've hired coaches to help me be a better public speaker. I've hired a coach to help me with my leadership skills. I've hired a coach to help me be a better marketer. I've hired a real estate coach to help me with my investments. I've hired a business coach to help my business grow. I've hired a coach to help me be a better coach.

By the way, if your coach doesn't have a coach, you need a new coach.

I'm sure I've hired more coaches throughout my lifetime, but those are the first ones who come to mind. You'll also notice that I've hired many coaches and not just one. When there is a particular area upon which I want to improve, I get a coach for that area.

I also want you to look at some of your favorite athletes. They have many coaches. Anyone who is performing at a high level has multiple coaches helping them every step of the way.

It's been said that *success leaves clues*. Just like elite athletes, if you want to perform at an elite level, you should hire a coach, too.

When hiring a coach, you must meet three criteria.

The first criteria are that you have to be teachable and coachable. You have to have an element of humility that you can learn from someone else and that you will act on their instruction.

The second criteria for hiring a coach is that you have chemistry with them. You want to work with someone you like and trust. You want to make sure your personalities gel well together.

The third criteria for hiring a coach is that they can get you results. You want a coach who isn't just going to talk to you about your feelings. A coach isn't a therapist. A coach doesn't heal the past. A coach focuses on the future and getting results.

Therapy certainly has its place, especially for healing the past and trauma that you may have experienced. I've certainly recommended therapy to some of my clients for things we've worked through, but for building the future, hiring a great coach is a must!

I want you to think about areas of your life in which you would like to improve. What areas of your life could you get a coach to speed up that particular result you are after?

Remember, a great coach will become your eyes and ears in providing you with a more accurate picture of your reality and will help you to establish better fundamentals. They'll guide your actions, breakdown processes and build you up better and faster.

Speed…And Safety. That's why we hire coaches.

Take Action:

- **Determine which skills you need to advance your life.**
- **Find a coach that can help you to reach your goals safer and faster.**

Chapter 21: The Difference that Makes the Difference

"A coach is someone who sees beyond your limits and guides you to greatness."
—**Michael Jordan**

What do Oprah Winfrey, Chuck Liddell, Andre Agassi, Von Miller, Danny Bonaduce, Nia Long, Metallica, Serena Williams, Bill Clinton, High Jackman, Eric Schmidt, Michael Jordan and Leonardo DiCaprio have in common?

They have all used coaches to help them on their path to greatness.

And this is just a shortlist of successful people who've hired a coach to help them achieve higher levels of success.

I've personally had the privilege of coaching professional athletes, artists, investors and everything in between. No matter what your path in life may be, we all can benefit from having a coach to show us the way.

I believe that success is 80% mindset and the other 20% is just the mechanics. For example, if you were a real estate investor,

20% of your job is the technical side of doing transactions. The other 80% is what happens inside your head.

It's in the 80% where we all need help, and that's what a great coach does is help you improve on the most important part—what goes on in your head. A great coach helps improve your performance, increases your knowledge, holds you accountable and gives you objective feedback.

Let me ask you this…Have you ever let fear hold you back? Have you ever felt lost? Have you ever felt as if you were not good enough? Do you want to have more focus? Do you have self-destructive habits that are preventing you from achieving your goals? Do you need a better system for time management?

If you said yes to any of those questions, I want to introduce you to *High Performance Coaching.*

What is High Performance Coaching?

High Performance Coaching is a form of personal and professional development to help you grow. It's focused on helping you become the best version of yourself and constantly find a new level of success in every area of life.

What does High Performance mean?

"*High Performance* means developing the behaviors and mindsets that help you consistently succeed beyond standard norms over the long-term while maintaining positive wellbeing and relationships."

In simple terms, *High Performance* is not about grinding, hustling and burning the midnight oil. It's not about working harder or working longer. It's not just for businesspeople or athletes. *High Performance* can help anyone from a mother, an executive, an artist or an entrepreneur to achieve success beyond the mediocre norms. It's for *anyone* wanting to break through to another level while maintaining positive wellbeing.

Would You Like My Help?

My goal is to help you break through any barriers that stop you from reaching your highest potential and performance. Together, we'll find ways for you to step into your best or highest self—the person you know you can and want to be.

As you work with my company or personally with me, you'll find yourself moving forward toward your goals and dreams faster than you ever thought possible. You will rapidly progress from where you are to where you want to be. And you will become increasingly able to make the big leaps you desire in all areas of your life. Plus, you'll feel inspired to take

189

positive and meaningful action every day. This allows you to live fully both at work and at home.

To find out which programs will work best for you, visit www.DelDenney.com to learn more.

I want to leave you with a quote from Aristotle: "We are what we repeatedly do. Excellence, then, is not an act, but a habit."

If it doesn't challenge you, it doesn't change you. I hope this book has given you some plays to use in your arsenal on your path to High Performance. The world needs High Performers. The world needs better leaders. I hope you commit to being a High Performer the world needs…that your family needs.

I'm here if you need me.

Your High Performance Coach,

Del Denney

About the Author

Del Denney is an author, coach and sought-after motivational speaker. By the age of 34 years old, he had traveled over one million miles conducting personal development seminars all across North America. Over the past 20 years, he has had the privilege of coaching entrepreneurs, TV celebrities, artists, and professional athletes. He lives in Indiana with his family, and you can visit him online at **DelDenney.com**

Printed in Great Britain
by Amazon

43118863R00116